Belief in Politics

Belief in Politics

Roy McCloughry

Edited by Huw Spanner

Hodder & Stoughton
LONDON SYDNEY AUCKLAND

British Library Cataloguing in Publication Data
A record for this title is available from the British Library

ISBN 0 340 65626 3

Typeset by Palimpsest Book Production Limited,
Polmont, Stirlingshire
Printed and bound in Great Britain by
Cox & Wyman Ltd, Reading, Berkshire

Hodder and Stoughton
A division of Hodder Headline PLC
338 Euston Road
London NW1 3BH

For my sister, Jean, with much love

Contents

Preface

This book started as an invitation from Huw Spanner, editor of *Third Way* magazine, to interview Tony Blair, MP, for a series of interviews he was running on opinion-formers in British culture entitled *High Profile*. This was followed by the interview, also contained in this collection, with Peter Lilley, MP. The response to both interviews was very positive and this led to the idea of interviewing other MPs. I was delighted when so many agreed to take part and talked with enthusiasm, and often with passion, about the issues which we face as a society. Those who are interviewed here are not representative of politics as a whole; there is only one woman MP and there are only politicians from the three major parties. Also a higher percentage of those interviewed have religious convictions or are interested in religious ideas than would be true of politics generally.

The interviews took place over nearly three years. In many cases I did two interviews to ensure that I had enough material. I need not have worried. The problem was that there was too much material. The interviews had to be drastically cut down. In order to make some sense of the task of editing I turned to Huw Spanner, who worked hard to cut the interviews to size while retaining their central ideas. I am grateful to him for the

Preface

time and effort he put into them while also busy editing a magazine.

Many people responded to my requests for ideas, information and possible questions. They are too numerous to name and I hope that they will accept my thanks in this form. Although I was the one who put the questions I was really a representative of many people "out there" who want to know what politicians "really think". However, I would particularly like to thank Sarah Holt and Kaja Ziesler, who worked hard on all aspects of the project, which would never have been completed without their skill and their tenacity. My thanks also to the politicians themselves who were willing to give me their time so generously, often in the middle of demanding schedules.

This book is not just interested in the "issues", it is also interested in politicians as people. Why did they enter politics, and what drives them? What kind of family upbringing did they have, and what values were they brought up to believe in? I decided to ask some of them similar questions so that comparisons could be made, but I also included several different questions to each politician. I tried to ignore issues which would provoke a predictable party response and also tried to avoid cross-party sniping. You must judge how successful I was! No doubt vast areas of important and urgent issues are left untouched, but I still hope that you find the end result fascinating to read.

Roy McCloughry
Nottingham, January 1996

Introduction

We are living through a period of unprecedented change in our society and in the world as a whole. Many of the issues we are currently facing were not dreamed of even thirty years ago. Global warming, AIDS, the fragmentation of the family, the rise of global markets and media are now familiar features of our culture. Yet we are uncertain of their implications for us. Such uncertainty about our destiny is at odds with the optimism which has usually been at the heart of modern thinking. We have become used to taking progress for granted rather than thinking of it as a distant possibility and assume that the application of human reason will overcome the problems which face us. In particular we believe that science and technology can find a way out of our most pressing dilemmas.

But we are not as sure as we once were. We are aware that our drive for progress may have been the cause of some of our ecological problems or may have been achieved at the expense of those who live in the Third World. Many Western societies are suffering from a crisis of purpose and meaning. As one commentator has put it, "Having constructed a society of unprecedented sophistication, convenience and prosperity, nobody can remember what it was supposed to be for."*

Introduction

At the very time when free markets are spreading all over the world and we should presumably be celebrating the wealth they create, we seem more reflective than joyful. The collapse of communism and state planning has led to the resolution of an ideological debate which has dogged this century. Social democracy and economic freedom of choice have clearly emerged as the victors. Yet this has not meant that critics of markets have been silenced. On the contrary, the demise of socialist economics has freed even right-wing thinkers from the spectre of being thought of as closet socialists if they criticise the markets. The result is real concern over their impact on us as a human community and on the world. This concern is the more heartfelt since the rapid globalisation of markets is affecting every culture in the world.

The main focus of this sense of apprehension is that markets may be good servants but they are bad masters. We live in a society in which economics seems to have taken over from science, which itself displaced religion, as the engine driving our hopes and aspirations. We see ourselves not so much as neighbours and friends, or even as citizens, but as consumers. Individual self-interest expressed through freedom of choice is at the heart of market decision-making, yet individualism is proving insubstantial as a building block for an entire society. We are not a collection of individuals but persons whose relationships and community life are essential to our identity as human beings. Economic efficiency and cost-effectiveness are not necessarily trustworthy custodians of the future of our culture.

* Clifford Longley in his introduction to Jonathan Sacks, *Faith in the Future*, Darton, Longman and Todd, London, 1995, p. x.

Belief in Politics

Perhaps it is in the area of human relationships that the poignancy of what is happening to us can be seen most clearly. For though human knowledge grows and we become more clever and skilful than we have ever been, human relationships do not change in the same way. Each generation needs love and respect, nurture and confidence, discernment and self-worth. If it is true that social cohesion is breaking down in Western societies, this is not due to a single cause. But it is a tragedy that at a time when we can accomplish so much in technical terms we are struggling to sustain our own human relationships.

We are a society which places a high value on human intimacy but cannot seem to generate the conditions necessary to enjoy it. As a result there is a nostalgia for community in our society and a growing hunger for a new approach to morality which will celebrate all that is good about life and provide the stability on which families and communities thrive. The word "community" represents a new emphasis on "belonging" as a characteristic of human relationships. It has also been taken up as one of the new buzzwords in contemporary political life. Communitarianism, which emphasises the importance of building strong human relationships and the importance of the voluntary sector in our national life, is now seen as an important new resource in politics. In a world where both individualism and collectivism have failed us perhaps it will help us move towards a new set of agendas by fusing together our need for love and justice in both relational and political terms.

The need for a new kind of politics underlies many of the interviews in this volume. In a world where corporations can be as powerful as governments, political authority is not as strong as it once seemed to be. Current

Introduction

European debate about the "pooling of sovereignty" in order to foster cooperation between nations is resisted by Britain, but one wonders how long this resistance can continue. Politicians are not as able as they once were to make decisions affecting national life without first considering their impact on global markets or their consequences in Brussels. Many of the touchstones of political life in the past seem now to be a fading dream. A sharply defined national identity has become a hostage to European fortunes. Similarly, egalitarian hopes for the welfare state are foundering on the costs of welfare provision now we are competing in open markets against countries with much lower costs. The historic commitments of both left- and right-wing politics are having to change in a world which is increasingly dominated by the emergence of Asia as the economic power of the twenty-first century.

Our own political parties had their identity shaped by a set of values very different from those which face us now. They have to change rapidly in order to address new issues without appearing to lose their roots and with them their traditional supporters. It is not an easy act to pull off. We are used to a fight between markets and nationalisation, individualism and collectivism, *laissez-faire* and big government, but now the parameters have changed. All parties now talk approvingly of markets and claim that in some way their policies provide us with both personal freedom and social justice. Recently, however, they have begun to adopt new ideas and language. The fight is on to be seen to be the party which best provides sustainable ecology, regional identity, community life, family values and even responsible parenting.

In the interviews collected in this book it is the similarity of ideas and attitudes rather than the difference which is striking. Politicians admit that the agenda is changing, that nobody knows what the future holds and that their visions overlap. They know that in many areas they do not have the power that they once did. They also know that the pressures on them are immense but that what they can achieve is often very modest, especially if they sit on the back benches. Yet each of the politicians interviewed in this book is dedicated to serving the public interest and works long hours to meet the needs of their constituents to the best of their ability. Perhaps our frustration with politicians is related more to absence of choice than to their personal performance. We live in a world where more choice implies more freedom, but as the messages of the parties seem to merge we are offered less choice at a time when the world and our place in it as a society are uncertain.

As a society we are in desperate need of a new vision. Those of us who are followers want leaders who will inspire us and fill us with hope. There is more to life than consumerism and individualism. We are aware that the language of politics is impoverished compared to our needs. We need not only justice but love, not only rights but forgiveness, not only welfare but healing. We do not want to survive, we want to flourish. Where do we go for such a vision in the modern world? What do we believe in which is bigger than us and our plans for our lives? The traditions which used to guide one generation after another are not considered to be relevant in a world where the only given is the pace of change. Institutions which embody those traditions are not trusted in the way they once were.

These agendas each find their place in this book. As the world changes so do politics and belief. Many of the politicians interviewed here have a religious belief of their own or are sympathetic to the Christian faith. What difference does that make to their lives and to their politics? Does being a Christian make any difference in a pluralistic world where tolerance is confused with indifference? Can we recover a set of spiritual values and beliefs which we can own, not as private individuals but as public truth for the community as a whole? These questions are important to our future as a community. There are no easy answers, but grappling with the questions is in itself a beginning, and it is that activity which best describes the purpose of this book.

David Alton

You have announced that you are not going to stand at the next election. After seventeen years as an MP, will you be sorry to leave the House?

I have been offered a couple of seats outside Liverpool, but simply being in Parliament is not what motivates me. I wouldn't have stood as a Liberal in the first place, in an inner-city seat we hadn't contested since 1950, if just getting elected was the be-all and end-all.

I will miss my constituents, and representing their interests. What I won't miss are the name-calling, the debunking, the Punch and Judy show that we call Prime Minister's Question Time. I certainly won't regret the rigidity of a place that almost regards you as a traitor if you dare suggest that something your party has said is wrong. There's something really rather unpleasant about that side of political life.

Nor will I miss the hypocritical way people boast of how democratic we are, when the system allows parties to be elected to absolute power with only 40 per cent of the vote. It is deceit when people talk about how weak all these continental democracies are because they have proportional representation.

1

I won't miss the xenophobia which you hear too often in the House. I won't miss the soundbites. I won't miss the people who tell me that if only they can climb one more rung on the ladder or strike one more deal, they'll be in a position to make some change in Parliament. The only change I notice is the one that occurs in them while they are there. It is very easy to get sucked in by the system.

That said, I still believe passionately in our parliamentary democracy, and I don't rule out standing for Parliament again at some time. If the Boundary Commissioners hadn't abolished me for the second time in ten years, maybe I would have been fighting the next election. But I would like a time for reflection and a chance to rethink my own political beliefs and where I want to go next. In the hurly-burly of politics you don't get a chance to do that. That is a regret I have, too, that there isn't much time for longer-term thinking.

Parliament doesn't look at the widest interests of the country; it rarely looks at issues on the merits of arguments. It usually looks at them on the basis of partisan positions, and a lot of that is to do with our electoral system, and the influence that party machines have over politicians. That will always be the nature of politics, to some extent. It is adversarial, a debate about ideas and principles, philosophy and ideology, and I wouldn't have it otherwise. There have to be disagreements, but it's how they're resolved that is the issue, and I don't think we have a very good procedure for doing that. Nor do we have a system that favours cooperation. I think it actually favours confrontation.

David Alton

How did you first get into politics?

I first got involved at school, albeit in a very modest way, by joining the Young Liberals. The 1967 Abortion Act had just gone through; internationally, people were starving to death in Biafra, the Americans were in Vietnam, Russian tanks had been rolling into Czechoslovakia. It was a very political time.

During my last year as a student in Liverpool, I stood for the local authority, in a run-down area where people had been neglected. I felt that I might put something back into that community in return for the hospitality I'd been given. It meant taking on the local political hierarchy, which was demolishing homes and removing people to places they didn't want to go to. I felt that was wrong. I got elected, and ultimately became chairman of the housing committee and deputy leader of the council.

We eventually stopped the bulldozers and declared the biggest round of housing action anywhere in the country. Many of those little streets of terraced houses were the ones that were to send me to Parliament in 1979. The only promises I made when I stood for Parliament were that I would live in the area and have advice centres every week, as I have done for twenty-four years now. I knew I could deliver on that.

I think that is part of the problem of politics, that we are always being urged to make slightly grander claims than our opponents. That leads to disillusionment in the end.

Your politics seems to be very concerned with morality, and yet people now see politics as, if anything, an immoral business.

I'm very proud that the first Liberal to represent my constituency – well, a Whig, really – was William Roscoe, who was elected in 1807. He cast his vote against slavery and had to pay a real price. When he returned to Liverpool he was pulled from the coach and beaten up, and he never came back to Parliament.

Another of my predecessors in Liverpool was Gladstone. We seem to think that the only things which will motivate people are tax cuts. Notwithstanding the fact that he was the first tax-cutting Chancellor, Gladstone was prepared to split his party down the middle on an issue of principle such as Irish Home Rule, even though it was going to send the party into the wilderness for fifteen years. These days, politicians would gasp at the idea of contesting a general election on such an issue.

I think the pressures in politics are very different now. People are far more influenced by general management committees and by lobby groups. I'm serving on the Privileges Committee at the moment, which is examining this cash-for-questions business. It's been very revealing to see how much people are in the pay of outside vested interests and how they serve those interests even before their constituents. So they come compromised in the first place. If you're owned by the tobacco industry, it's not surprising when you oppose any ban on advertising. And that's immoral and unethical. Morality is too often equated with questions of sex.

I'm not opposed to people having outside business

4

interests; I do want to see a broadly based Parliament. But I am opposed to people procuring new financial interests by virtue of being Members. That's altogether different. And I would like to see every candidate at a general election being required to declare their interests. If someone has 250 directorships and fifty consultancies, people can judge for themselves whether that person would have the time to represent them.

People who ask questions for money should be subject to criminal charges, as they would be in local government. Words like "privilege" epitomise what's wrong with the stuffy way Parliament works. It all dates back to 1542, when the Speaker was fighting to maintain the privilege of MPs to speak out on behalf of their constituents and their consciences. Today, MPs seem to think they have the privilege to be lobbyists and consultants, and to earn huge sums of money in addition to their parliamentary salaries. If they had to disclose everything, they would be a bit more careful about the interests in which they got involved.

How has your Christian commitment affected your political priorities?

I've never made any secret of it. It determines my agenda.

There are plenty of issues which I am interested in but on which many other people speak very eloquently and knowledgeably. There is no need to replicate what they are doing. On the other hand, there are issues that I think are marginalised, like the pro-life issue. For me, it is the supreme human-rights issue: the very right to life for the most vulnerable human beings of all. Also, there is a school of thought which says that if you are against abortion, you must be some sort of right-wing, misogynist, fundamentalist bigot. I totally dispute that, so it's even more important for people like me to be identified with it.

Barely a week would pass without my tabling questions in the House of Commons about pro-life issues. I helped Dame Jill Knight move her successful amendment this year to stop the use of aborted baby girls in fertility treatment by the plundering of their ovaries. In the last twelve months I've been very active in trying to stop Dutch-style euthanasia laws being introduced here. And I've raised the issue of sex selection and the continued use of amniocentesis to weed out the handicapped. They have the right to be born.

If we measure political success not in terms of the Dow Jones index or the pound against the Deutschmark, but in terms of what's happening to human beings, we would come to radically different conclusions about the health of our nation. The Greens did us a great service during the Seventies in adopting exactly that kind of approach to environmental issues.

I think that what we're doing to the human being, from conception to death, should be a central question. There's a danger for so-called anti-abortionists of being so obsessed with the rights of the unborn that they forget that life doesn't end at birth. You must also be concerned about what happens to the child on the other side of birth. There are 46,000 children on child-protection registers in Britain, for fear of physical or sexual abuse; we've got 98,000 children running away from home every year, and we don't even keep a national computerised register. We have 100,000 young people addicted to drugs.

Are all these social problems – drug abuse, homelessness, abortion – consequences of the breakdown of the family?

I'm not sure that the family should be the starting point. I start from the proposition that when a society loses respect for life, it loses everything. Indeed, I would argue that the degradation of life in society generally, the lack of respect we have for one another today, in many ways stems from the cavalier approach we have to the genesis of life.

The family is the most basic building block of society, but the neighbourhood community also is crucial. The country is a community; so is Europe. (You could say it hasn't delivered in some respects, just as family life itself has gone off the rails, but the vision was the right one.) How do you restore that sense of community at every level? In the west of Ireland, where my mother comes from, they say of community that it's in the shelter of each other's lives that the people live.

I think that government, for one thing, should have to produce family impact statements, in the same way as they produce environmental impact statements, for every single line of policy. If the Budget had to detail its effect on the family, we'd have a very different debate on it, but it's almost an irrelevance. The Conservative Party said it cared about the family, but it's now financially better not to be married, and the Government is introducing proposals actually to make divorce easier, and it has done very little to secure the position of children in society.

What do you think has caused the demise of the family?

During the Fifties and Sixties, a whole range of factors began to have a pretty massive impact on the family. Personal mobility had increased. Slum clearance began to break up many communities. Television started to be available in people's homes all over the country. The sexual revolution was under way. In addition, you had Harold Macmillan promoting the idea that "having it good" was where life was at. All that became corrosive of some of the better values we had in this country.

But I'm not one of those who hark back to some mythical golden age. I think these things go in cycles. The Thirties, for instance, were a pretty desperate time for people. You can hardly pretend that was a golden age in the immediate run-up to the Second World War. There have always been pressures on family living. Some of them were concealed rather better in the Victorian age, maybe, than today.

The issue for us is: do we want to allow the continued destruction of the family, or do we want to try to make it easier for people to stay together? Easier divorce laws, for instance, hold little appeal for me. Reducing the money available to organisations like Relate seems an extraordinarily stupid thing to do when you should be encouraging people who do want to persevere.

I think we may be beginning to see the pendulum swing back again. There is a sense that it's all gone too far: the destruction of family life has not brought the liberation people assumed. People can survey the wreckage around them and realise this is not a particularly good way of living.

Is there a simple solution? Are you one of those who say, "If only we were to rediscover religion"?

I think that religious values help to weave a nation together. The massive political changes that occurred after the Napoleonic Wars, the advent of Chartism, the demand for suffrage, the emancipation of Jews and Catholics and slaves, the abolition of the national lottery, the great Reform Act of 1832, stemmed, I believe, from William Wilberforce's call for a moral change in the country. He wasn't just opposed to slavery: he said (in a rather quaint phrase) he wanted to reform "the manners and morals of the age".

What did that flow out of? Out of religious revival. You can trace it back, I think, primarily to John Wesley. The people who moved events then were the Evangelical Movement and the Anglo-Catholics. And that's what we must look for today. Religious revival is a prerequisite to all the other things that I hope for.

There has to be more to life than unfettered individualism and consumerism. But not everyone who has a strong family life is necessarily a believer, and equally many believers find their marriages run into trouble. So I don't think it is as simple as that; but it certainly helps if at the outset of your marriage you take a solemn vow and believe you are also making a commitment to God.

If you eliminate God from national life, it has disastrous consequences for society. We have become very self-sufficient in this country. We feel we don't need God any more. He may have been needed in past generations, but he's no longer relevant. We are wedded to consumerism, choice and individualism but people will once again search for values beyond the immediate price tag.

My instinct is that people are beginning to rediscover that there is life beyond themselves. I don't get so many people now at student meetings, for instance, telling me they're atheists or agnostics. Quite a lot tell me they're into the New Age. We've just seen the appointment of the first pagan chaplain at a British university. I think that's symptomatic. People are trying to find something spiritual, something beyond themselves, but they are bypassing the Church.

I certainly think the institutional Church is failing us. It is still a scandal for Christianity that we are as divided as we are. It's another breakdown in family, if you like, that within our own Church family we have these terrible, long-term disputes unresolved. Why should the world take us seriously?

One way in which Christians have come together is in the Christian Democratic movement. What does it mean to be a Christian Democrat, though? David Hunt seems to be one, and he's a senior Conservative.

I would have quite a lot in common with David Hunt and Chris Patten, for instance. I don't find myself a million miles removed from a lot of the things they believe in. We're in different political parties because there is no Christian Democrat party in this country, and I would not

10

David Alton

be comfortable inside the modern Conservative Party. I would be interested to know how David Hunt can feel comfortable in it.

The ideals of Christian Democracy can be traced back to the immediate aftermath of the war, after the abject failure of Christians in Germany to engage in public and political life. They had privatised their faith and opted out of any civic responsibility. The coming together of evangelical Protestants and orthodox Catholics after the war was to provide a new political settlement for Germany and, indeed, every other Western European country in one way or another.

The Movement for Christian Democracy in this country has set out its principles very clearly. It believes in social justice, respect for life, reconciliation, active compassion, empowerment and good stewardship. It sets the human personality at the heart of its concerns, and it believes in an approach based on community. It has championed issues from video violence to the use of British aid to sterilise and possibly perform abortions on women in China. If someone says they're a Christian Democrat, it's there to encourage and stimulate them and to challenge and, if necessary, rebuke them if they fall short of those political ideals. I think there is a need for a movement that brings together people from all the disparate traditions. That in itself helps because it enables Christians to feel less isolated, to exchange ideas and to go and influence their own parties.

People's view of Christian Democracy is sullied by Christian Democratic parties on the Continent, which have often been in power for many years and, like any other party, have become corrupted by that power. You've got to have a very realistic view of political parties. They're not the communion of saints.

11

Do you foresee a new partnership between Catholics and evangelicals in British politics?

The close cooperation between evangelicals and Catholics started over the abortion issue. But all of us agreed when we got together that it would be absurd, and really rather sad, if that was the only issue around which we could unite. As we got to know one another, there were other things about which we agreed, and we have forged a genuinely and consistently pro-life agenda together.

In Liverpool I can see the real value of that achievement; and in Northern Ireland as well, thank God, and not before time. Christians must recognise that the enemy is no longer denominationalism or sectarianism but secularism. That will be where orthodox Christians are going to find themselves standing together. That's where the old animosities will disappear. Those values are needed beyond our denominations. A new civic alliance which redresses the imbalance between rights and duties is now needed.

Do you think we are seeing a convergence between Labour and the Conservatives?

Yes. I was talking to a Government minister recently who told me she didn't mind entirely if they lost the election because they'd won the battle of ideas and the Labour Party now stood for all the things she stood for. I never expected to hear this particular minister saying that sort of thing. If that's the perception now, that the two parties are actually saying the same thing and individualism has won all the arguments, this is quite depressing.

12

I'm not sure that it has gone as far as that. If you read
Andrew Marr or Melanie Phillips, David Selbourne or
Amitai Etzione, there are clearly people around who
see the urgent need to return to a greater sense of
community. Tony Blair seems to realise that the most
important community of all is the family, and I think he
does genuinely believe in its preservation as a building
block for society, but clearly a lot of people in the Labour
Party don't, so there will be a struggle over these ideas in
the next few years.

In the vote for the secularisation of Sunday, Tony
Blair took the lead as home affairs spokesman, even
voting against my own amendment (which was ultimately
successful) to keep Easter and Christmas Day as special
days. I find that very hard to accept when someone is
arguing that you must seek a more responsible society
that cares about the quality of life in the community.

*And yet Labour politicians are talking increasingly in
terms of responsibility.*

I think the Labour Party is having a partial revelation,
which may turn out to be a much better beginning than
perhaps it appears. I hope it does. But it may only be
allowed to go so far. In the area of public justice, they
are quite strong, but when it comes to matters of personal
responsibility, they still hanker after the individual's right
to do as they please.

My assumption is that the Labour Party will win
the next election. We will see little expenditure on
health and education (which for me would be very
high priorities) because they've refused to give any

promises about increasing taxes. What we will see is constitutional change, because it doesn't cost much and it gives the impression of reform, and anyway it might be able to ensure that Labour get another term in government subsequently. I think they will act particularly on devolution in Northern Ireland and Scotland, and on freedom of information, and also on a referendum on PR.

The other area where they will act will be on social issues, because that costs little but it will placate the left. Everything from euthanasia to extending the Abortion Act to Northern Ireland, and possibly legalisation of drugs, which a lot of people in that party, and indeed in my own, support. I think that agenda will surface very strongly, and people who have voted for them will feel extraordinarily disillusioned because they didn't realise what they were getting. But in the kingdom of the blind, the one-eyed man is king.

Are you pessimistic about the future of British politics?

I hope that we're going to see a movement away from the kind of politics we've had, but my suspicion is that the straitjacket in which the present political parties are tied will not allow that to happen.

That's why, for me, the key is a referendum on PR. Let the people decide to change the voting system and that then creates diversity. If there's diversity within our system, there's no reason at all why something like a Christian Democratic alternative should not be successful. And that would include among its principles belief in community, human personality, subsidiarity and solidarity – all things that I think are crucial to the survival of civilisation.

Quite a lot of people would support such ideals, including existing members of the Conservative Party, who, after all, will just have suffered a defeat. Men like Chris Patten, who will have just returned from Hong Kong, will surely not be able to stomach the right-wing xenophobia of people like Michael Portillo, who will probably have become the leader of the party. In those circumstances, we could well see a fragmentation, as we saw in the Labour Party in 1979, and a new kind of politics emerging. That would be truly exciting.

That would force change within all the other parties, too. The socialists within the Labour Party might decide to go their own way: with PR they could be free of the straitjacket, because they could survive on their own with 15 or 20 per cent of the popular vote. The Liberal Democrats would be subsumed by the rump of "new" Labour. Then you would have political parties from the right-wing, a British nationalist rump of the Tory Party, a Christian Democratic party, a Social Democratic party and Arthur Scargill's Socialist Party. You would actually then have the variations that most people look for in politics, which don't really exist at the moment. So I think we're living in interesting political times.

Biography

David Alton was educated at Campion School, Horn-church, and Christ's College, Liverpool. From 1972 to 1979 he was a teacher, specialising mainly in children with special educational needs.

Belief in Politics

In 1972, at the age of twenty-one, he was elected to Liverpool City Council and the following year to Merseyside County Council. He contested the seat of Liverpool Edge Hill in both the general elections of 1974, and in 1979 was elected as Liberal Member of Parliament for Edge Hill.

In 1983 he held the new seat of Liverpool Mossley Hill.

He has been Liberal Party spokesperson on housing, the environment, home affairs, overseas aid and local government, and Alliance spokesperson on Northern Ireland. He was Liberal Chief Whip, Parliamentary Aide to David Steel, and a member of the Select Committee on the Environment. He is currently a member of the Committee of Privileges.

He was a founder member of the Epiphany Group, and co-sponsor of the All Party Movement for Christian Democracy.

His publications include *What Kind of Country?* (1987), *Whose Choice Anyway?* (1988), and *Faith in Britain* (1991).

He is married and has one daughter and two sons.

Two interviews with David Alton were conducted on 12 December 1994 and 24 October 1995.

Paddy Ashdown

Why are you in politics?

I often ask myself that. I was in the Foreign Service, and my wife and I lived a very enjoyable life in a big house on the shore of Lake Geneva. We went boating with the kids, and skiing in the mountains, and we had our own yacht. And quite suddenly, in 1974, we both agreed it wasn't enough. We saw our country in crisis and we wanted to put our lives into something we thought mattered. I don't say this in any sort of "Aren't I wonderful?" way, but I've always been driven by the idea of service. I don't pretend there is any altruism in it: it gives me satisfaction.

So we embarked on this curious trail which took me eight years to get elected, and two periods of unemployment and salaries half what I was getting in the Foreign Service. It's what we wanted to do: we've never regretted it. I took risks, including with my family. People might well say some of them were irresponsible, but, thank God, it has ended up with me in a job which I absolutely adore, which turns out to be the job for which the rest of my life was an apprenticeship.

Belief in Politics

You come over as a politician who has a moral vision rather than as someone who just wants to tinker with the system. How did your family background shape you?

I came from a very loving family, which was run, I think, according to the values of Christendom, if not of Christianity. My mother was a strong Protestant and my father, whom I respected immensely, a rather casual Catholic. She gave the family stability, weight and centre; he gave it adventure and life and challenge, and made us all argue a great deal. His values still drive me, values about decency, truth and honesty and, in particular, courage. He used to say, and I believe it strongly, that for a politician the ultimate quality is moral courage. Without it, all the other gifts you have fade away.

My family has been attended by tragedy. I'm the eldest of seven, of whom three have died, one in an accident, two from disease. And then, when I was eighteen, I watched my father go through business failure and bankruptcy, which was for him a terrible shame. And my family were taken from me: they went out to Australia. So an immense sense of insecurity is part of my make-up.

And, last, because I was brought up in Northern Ireland and across the religious divide, I understand the importance of tolerance. This is the very heart of democracy. Without pluralism, democracy will tend towards tribalism and conflict, the celebration of Me and the tight vision of Us rather than the incorporating vision of Us.

Paddy Ashdown

Does pluralism always mean the lowest common denominator, or can it respect strong voices?

Pluralism is meaningless if it is the pluralism of the lowest common denominator. It's pointless if I diminish my beliefs until they are not a challenge to yours. I want to see a strong, red-blooded set of beliefs which challenge and question each other. I can't see any way you can get human progress without that.

But I also want people to have respect and tolerance for others' points of view precisely because they are dangerous if you challenge them. Now, how you get there is tricky. Bosnia is the second example, after Northern Ireland, of what are going to be the great scourges of our age, which are fundamentalism and tribalism. That's why I go back to Bosnia twice a year: I am horrified by how flimsy the veil is that separates us from the brutes and how easily it is torn down, and once that veil is torn down, it is almost impossible to put it back again. People who were next-door neighbours do unspeakable things to each other on the basis that my Us is different from yours.

Do you tend to see religion as a sectarian thing?

Yes. I note that the best things have been done in the name of religion, but the worst things have been done in its name as well.

I count myself a Christian but I get uncomfortable when somebody says, "Are you Protestant or a Roman Catholic?" That's not the kind of Christian I am. I pray every night, I believe in a Christian God, but it's an encompassing God that recognises and understands.

Belief in Politics

There's a great phrase that my father often used, that every person should have the right to search for the right. I would defend that right, but I would argue to the bitter end with anyone who tells me they've found it, because those who believe they have found the truth have also found an excuse for intolerance and oppression towards those who have found a different truth.

The search for the truth is more important to me than pretending you have found it. And that reads across to religion. I conduct my life according to a code of Christian values, which I happen to believe is a very good code for our age; but my belief in God is separate from that. I won't say it is unconnected, but it transcends my value structure.

My religion is a private affair. I have not been able to go into churches very easily because of my experiences in Northern Ireland. My wife often says she wouldn't be at all surprised to find me drawn back to one of the main religions before the end of my life, but I am not ready for that yet. There is a great poem of Francis Thompson, "The Hound of Heaven":

> I fled him, down the nights and down the days,
> I fled him, down the arches of the years,
> I fled him, down the labyrinthine ways
> Of my own mind.

What positive things do you see in religion?

The job of the Church is to be a moral arbiter, to say, "We believe this to be bad." Who else will do it in our society? I'm a firm believer that establishment is a very bad thing for the Church and the state. If the Church is too entangled with the state, it becomes too involved in the pragmatic and the practical. If the Church will not fly the banner for morality, you may be sure politicians won't because we are far too much engaged in the grubby business of getting elected and dealing with practicalities. The more I hear the Church taking positions on what it regards as moral issues and showing compassion as a counterbalance to this hard-driven practicality of politics, the happier I am.

You say how easily people can become brutes, and yet you believe in people.

Yes, and in the great revelation that "The proper study of mankind is man." The individual matters and has the right to freedom and deserves to be dignified.

It is my starting point that people are worthy to be trusted. I don't know if they are good. They are probably not; original sin is a very powerful motivator. But if you trust them, they will usually rise to it. Look at the firms that are succeeding in the global marketplace. They have stripped down the hierarchies and they're networking. In politics, we have lovingly preserved the hierarchies. But you have got to have the courage to let people and communities make the wrong decisions.

That isn't to say you can't be let down. Of course you can. It doesn't mean that you haven't given power to people who have become vile and corrupt and deeply destructive. I have done that too. But I've said to people, "You really ought to be in politics," and persuaded them to stand, and I've watched people who two years ago were saying, "Oh, I couldn't," take charge of committees, take decisions, develop their own ideas. That's what gives me a kick in politics, more than anything else. You watch them grow. It is like a flower blossoming. It makes my heart stop whenever I see it.

What motivates such people?

I can't answer that. I know what my motivation is and I suspect it's theirs as well. Nietzsche said: "The strong man helps the weak, not through altruism but through superabundance of power."

I love my surgeries. It is the one day in the week when I feel I'm doing a good job of work. But I know that I am doing this for other people because it satisfies me. I look in the mirror every day and I think, "You are not doing this for altruism, you are not doing it because you are good; you are doing it because it is what you want, you are doing it for you." And it is very important that you hang on to that.

I think that most of us who go about "doing good for others" (shocking phrase) would say that if you asked them. They do it because they want to, because they enjoy it.

When Margaret Thatcher appealed to self-interest, we got individualism. What are you going to appeal to in people to bring about the kind of world you want?

I believe there are two parts of the human psyche, the Me part and the Us part, and they both have to be satisfied.

22

The convincing political creed has to answer both. We all know how destructive egoism is.

Politics has become a thing you do by numbers. This Government is not a government, it's an administration, and rather a bad one at that. I will tell you why: because we live in an age of the death of isms. Communism, socialism, capitalism, they are all dead. For what ism, except perhaps fascism and nationalism, would you now stand on the barricade and risk your life?

Now I can see the shape of something new emerging, and it has a strong moral quotient. And I can tell you what it's about: it's about citizenship, about community, which is about duties and responsibilities as well as rights. It's about the concept that we cannot pass on to future generations the environmental costs we generate in this. It's about internationalism, about understanding that we have to work together with other nations. The concepts of international good and evil are things which ought to have political effect.

I can see all the ingredients, but we can't find a name, and in politics something does not exist until it has a name. The struggle at present is to codify that set of ideas.

Won't it be difficult to get people to embrace this vision for themselves? The last decade has turned us into a nation of consumers.

Is that actually true? It's what we believe to be true, and what politicians have responded to, but I wonder if it is true. None of us are giving people a clear lead. None of us are actually telling the truth, and, what's more, they know we don't tell the truth, they know it. And we know we don't tell the truth, but we persist in illusions and lies.

The two great political lies are the Conservative lie, "Vote us in and your taxes will always be lower", and the Labour lie, "Give me your vote and I will give you back your job." It's absolute nonsense, and I think that is why Britain is in a profoundly demoralised state. People are saying, "For God's sake, somebody, tell us the truth!"

But it doesn't have to be like that. What are the things that have changed our lives? Is it government that caused us to see the importance of Third World hunger? No, it was pop music, Band Aid and all that. And it changed a culture. I am struck by the incapacity of political parties to communicate in ways that move people because they always want to depend on people's baser instincts, and the ease with which artists can move people because they are prepared to appeal to something a bit higher.

Politics is now being conducted against a different background. For what I call the Atlantic-shore democracies, the politics of the last thousand years have been against a background of rising prosperity. That's easy. The politician's contract with the people is "Give me your vote and I will give you the goodies." But if we are looking at a period of declining aspirations, in relative terms if not absolute ones, as we see the rise of alternative class structures and the shift of economic power to the Pacific Basin, then the whole nature of politics has to change. It's got to. Instead of a paternalism that says, "We'll deliver the goodies to your home. Just let us go on running the country," it has to be "Look, we've got a joint problem and we have got to solve it. We can do it together."

Paddy Ashdown

So how do you see the nature of politics changing?

The problem is that we have the nation-state and the individual but we have no intermediary structures in between, and we have to create those. The nation-state is no longer sufficiently relevant to carry all our Us's. It's no longer a sufficient context for us to understand our identity. I am not saying that it is somehow going to wither away and not matter. It is an element of our identity and the means by which we express our influence, which will always be very important. But it is no longer good enough to wave the flag and say, "I am British," because we are more than that. When it comes to me expressing my identity, it is not exclusively a nation-state identity. I happen to feel an Irishman because I was born there. I happen to feel a West Countryman because I live there. I happen to feel British, and proud of it. And I happen to feel a European. This is part of the pluralism of identity that we have all got to be able to attach ourselves to.

But those of us who believe that the solution is something to do with community (which is a very difficult concept) ought also to realise that there are limits to the community. If you devolve power, you may create the very sense of cultural purity that will drive a tribalist approach.

For instance, I have always believed in the devolution of power to a Scottish parliament. I think the Scottish nation has a right to an element of self-government. But there is no doubt that those who argue that case in the Scottish National Party are now arguing it from a tribalist view, and even more so in Wales, where the nationalist movement has really tipped over the edge.

In the past, the state has been the arbiter of civil rights, of fairness and justice. Now, you cannot devolve that power unless you are absolutely sure that the organisation to which you are devolving it is pluralist and tolerant in nature: otherwise, it will tip over into tribalism. That's why, for me, education plays such an important part.

Second, you still have to have an overarching structure. Look at what's happened in Europe, for instance: the rise of nationalism, of fascism, of tribalism, not just in Germany but with Jean-Marie Le Pen in France. The nation-state is no longer capable of containing it; indeed, in many ways it is the vehicle for it. In my view, the biggest idea for the next century is to create something strong enough to be able to contain those pressures and to give an alternative identity.

Do you share the view that our nation is in decline?

It seems to me unquestionably true that we are a nation of declining morality. People seem less and less to have a code to live by, a light to follow, a path to pursue, that defines their actions and the limits of those actions.

But I don't think that's their fault. It's ours. If this is the age without isms, if the trumpet will not sound a confident note, it is hardly surprising.

In many ways the Church too has failed. I don't want to see the Church lay down hard, wooden dogma. Dogma is a very difficult thing to cope with. But let us recognise that if we have lost our way, as I think we probably have, it is not "the people's" fault. Moss Side is not just an indictment of the people who do it, though they have responsibility, we can't deny that, but an indictment of the rest of us, too.

I think I've got a fair idea where the solution to this lies, but I can't give you a grid reference for it yet or a very clear path to it, though I hope we will manage to work one out.

A lot of people will feel uncomfortable with the idea of a world dominated by transnational companies and trading blocs.

I feel uncomfortable about it too, and no doubt I would feel uncomfortable if I was at sea in a boat and a storm was over the horizon. The question is not "How do we avoid it?", because we can't, but "How do we cope with it?"

I am also deeply worried about the immorality of the international system as it currently is. The frightening thing is that institutions based in the nation-state seem to be on the decline, and the institutions that are flourishing are those that ignore national borders. Some are benign, or potentially so. The internet seems to me to be. It can't be a bad thing to pass round information, though it may be passed round for the wrong reason. The United Nations and the ideal of international action in the preservation of international law is benign. The others are not necessarily immoral but amoral. The commodity market, the pop-music culture are not morally founded, and their capacity to be run in a way which is deeply destructive is therefore very worrying. The transnational corporations, some of which are now bigger than nation-states, have no loyalty, no founding morality, and they are powerful enough to do anything. That poses a huge question. Are we prepared to let this continue? This vast international money-go-round is one of the great destabilising factors that can crash economies and wreck people's lives. It's very difficult to control it now, but what are we going to do? Are we prepared to go on letting transnational corporations invest in this country and take out all the profits, and then pull the plug out and move somewhere else? Is it a good thing, a wise thing, to do? The world has to face up to how it will limit the behaviour of these people. It's not going to be easy, but you've got to do it.

Do you see the market itself as amoral or immoral?

I think it is just like any other power. If something has power – and you have power, I have power, the state has power, newspapers have power, trades unions have power – the first question you have to ask is: "What are the limits of that power?" The only thing that doesn't apply to is God. And the market is not God.

You have said that we should cut taxation on the things we want more of, such as income and labour, and raise it on the things we want less of, such as pollution. What did you mean by that?

It is immoral, as well as politically wrong, for us to incur environmental costs today which we will hand on to future generations. We have to cost the environment into the economy, and taxation is a way of doing that. Incidentally, by so doing, you would encourage a virtuous circle of efficiency and conservation, which at present is not encouraged because we are into conspicuous

28

consumption. But there is a limit to how much you can use this technique. You have to invest in the supply side. The marketplace won't. It won't invest in education; how can it? It can't accurately judge what the value of it is. And by and large the marketplace will not invest in the sort of infrastructure you need. I often quote Robert Reich, who says that in the era of footloose capital, the global market, the only things that will remain rooted within a nation are the intellectual capital of its people and the nature of its infrastructure, and so you better invest in those two.

In many ways, Hong Kong is a remarkable model of what Britain might like to become, and on the wall of the Department of Trade and Industry office there is a big board which says, "Private enterprise: public investment". They told me: "That's our slogan in Hong Kong, because we understand that this is a partnership. Unless we make the public investment in the infrastructure and education that industry needs, private enterprise can't flourish. But we won't take over private enterprise, we are there to create the backdrop." And throughout Hong Kong everybody understands that.

The role of government is to provide the public investment that is necessary for private enterprise and for private lives to be lived most effectively and efficiently. That, it seems to me, is the important thing. Now, you could maintain the overall level of tax burden in Britain but change the taxation base, so that you were taxing more pollutants and finite raw materials, and you could put that money straight back into the infrastructure – for instance, the transport and communications infrastructure – and in effect you would be creating a virtuous circle towards greater efficiency. I think this is an idea which we have to try and push forward as hard as we can.

Belief in Politics

How do you see the future?

I think the world will be much more regionally based.
One of the worst effects of that, incidentally, will be
a diminution in free trade and a rise in protectionism,
not nation-to-nation but region-to-region. We will have
to have some concept of international power that is
capable of upholding international law and individual
civil rights, not for moral reasons but because that is
the only way we will have peace in a world that is
increasingly interdependent, where a nuclear gangster
could threaten us all.

I think you will have quite strong regional bodies, and
Europe will be the first and, hopefully, the most powerful.
If the European institutions are to succeed, they will have
to be more powerful where at present they don't have
enough power, and less powerful where they have too
much. Preserving the cultural diversity of Europe is
absolutely vital, I think, and the nation-states will be a
primary way of doing that. But within nation-states there
will be a greater sense of regionalism, and so we will have
a much broader and more even settlement of power.

*What would your immediate priorities be if you were in
power?*

If I could do three things, I would invest in education
because it is the key that unlocks everything, not just
economically. It creates self-reliance, it makes stable
societies, it gives people power in their own hands.
It's the one gift you can give them that no one can
ever take away.

30

Second, I would take the power of Parliament, this wretched, out-of-date museum piece, and spread it around Britain and let people run their own lives.

The third thing I would do would lock both of those together. I would invest something like £6 billion (which is two years of British Telecom's research budget) to build an internet capable of connecting every single person in this country to all the knowledge in the world. That is what it is capable of doing.

Do those three things and no one will be able to stop the change that would follow because people would have the power and, above all, the information necessary to change this whole thing.

Biography

Paddy Ashdown was born in 1941 and educated at Bedford School, where he followed his father, his grandfather and his great-grandfather. It was there that he acquired the nickname Paddy. (He was christened Jeremy John Durham.)

In 1959 he joined the Royal Marines and he saw active service as a commando officer in Borneo and the Persian Gulf. In 1965 he commanded a Special Boat Section in the Far East and, in 1967, went to Hong Kong to study Mandarin Chinese full-time. In 1970, as a captain, he was given command of a company in Belfast – at that time, the youngest Marine officer to be given such an appointment since the war.

He left the forces in 1971 to join the Diplomatic Service and worked as First Secretary in the British Mission to the UN in Geneva.

In 1976 he moved to Somerset, where he took a job as a commercial manager with the Westlands Group. He stood as the Liberal candidate for Yeovil in the 1979 general election and in 1983 won the seat with a majority of 3,600. He was soon asked to speak for the Liberals on trade and industry affairs.

In 1987 he became Alliance spokesperson on education and science and in 1988 Liberal Democrat spokesperson on Northern Ireland. In July 1988 he was elected leader of the Liberal Democrats, comfortably beating Alan Beith with 71.9 per cent of the vote. He was appointed a Privy Councillor six months later.

In 1994 he travelled extensively in the UK researching for his book *Beyond Westminster*. His previous writings include *Citizen's Britain* (1989).

This interview was conducted on 3 February 1995.

Alan Beith

*Many politicians say they're not in it for the power or the
kudos, but to work for change. Is that true of you?*

One reason why there are relatively large numbers of
Christians in politics must be that there is an impulse
to service. It's just something you believe in. I never sat
down and said, "What should my career be? I want to
be a politician." It arose out of just getting involved in
voluntary and public activity.

It's frustrating for us Liberal Democrats, having been
kept out of power so much. But I'd like to feel that I've
changed the way people view the Member of Parliament
in my constituency. People regard their MP as someone
they can readily approach and put their views to.

I hope I've helped with the tremendous growth of the
Liberal Democrat Party. This is a very different party, in
terms of its strength of numbers, from the one I was active
in in the Sixties and Seventies. When I attend conference
debates now as home affairs spokesman, I am constantly
being contacted by Liberal Democrat police-authority
chairmen, fire-committee chairmen, leading figures from
all over the country. This party is now much more
involved in the running of communities than it was
when I joined it. At local-authority level, there are

thousands of councillors, particularly in the southern part of the country, giving people an alternative to what had become a sterile choice between the two other parties.

And we've kept promoting ideas as well, drawing on a strong tradition. And there are all sorts of campaigns that you work on which matter, ranging from the very specific, like campaigning successfully to get disposable syringes for diabetics, through to having some success, I think, in helping to halt the advance of nuclear power.

Does it make any difference to your politics that you are a Christian?

It's one of the things which inspire me, and it leads me to tackle things I might otherwise prefer not to. It also provides the basic framework of my philosophy.

Quite often, my Christianity leads me to take a particular view on an issue, but other Christians may differ quite sharply from me – on overseas aid, for example, or abortion or war. It's not unusual. The importance you attach to the issue may be shared, but the conclusions you reach may not be.

What are the moral issues in our country that concern you most?

The disconnection between people, the loss of a sense of mutual responsibility in the community as a whole and also, dramatically, within families. Many parents don't abandon their children, but they get themselves into a situation where they can't exercise their responsibility very effectively. Materialism, and the emphasis the Thatcher years placed on getting what you can for yourself and perhaps, if you're very successful, giving a little away to others. Violence, and the disregard of others which it represents. I think it's going to take us some time to reassert other values without destroying initiative and enterprise, which are clearly important.

Some of the things are the result of economic change, which has caused disruption in societies throughout the centuries. Some are the result of various public policies which attempted to satisfy one aspiration and destroyed another – such as rehousing whole communities in out-of-town estates to get rid of bad housing, which contributed to this disconnection of people from their families.

Again, some very sincere people genuinely believed that the 1967 Abortion Act was dealing with the evil of backstreet abortions, but the effect was, I think, to remove the public and legal recognition that abortion is killing unborn children. That, I think, was a serious loss of a basic ethical framework.

Who should we look to to solve these problems? Politicians? The schools? The Churches?

We do what we can do. Other organisations and individuals do what they can do.

You can't legislate or administer some of these problems out of existence. Sometimes people write to me individually, as if by my vote in the House of Commons I could abolish sin or get rid of particular social evils which they don't like or behaviour they disapprove of. Nevertheless, I would be worried if we weren't being challenged to do more than we think we can. That would be a sign of a loss of prophetic vision, which will always be reaching a little further than seems possible, maybe a lot further. I think that Christian organisations and individuals are showing a renewed determination to project their values through whatever political party they feel comfortable with and to challenge all political parties.

There are various things you can do through the powers of Parliament and government. You can try to make sure the basic services are available which make people less likely to get into trouble. You can try to organise communities in the way most conducive to good community life. You can try to support and not destroy families, by the way your tax and benefit system works and by your housing policies. And you can punish serious offences.

Do you think the Church is sufficiently involved in these issues? Or is it too involved, when it should be concentrating on giving us a spiritual lead?

I can hardly say that Christian groups are not addressing problem areas in society. I think they are. There's an awful lot going on. Some people get a picture of a Church obsessed with social issues, largely because newspapers only report the sayings of Church leaders if they are on political or social issues – unless they're denying the birth of Christ.

A lot of nonsense is talked about this, especially by

Conservative politicians. Whenever Church leaders say anything controversial on any social or political question, they tend to say, "The Church should concentrate on spiritual things. That's what's wrong with it, it only thinks about politics." It just happens that the only thing they notice is what the Church occasionally says on social and political issues. They entirely disregard the pastoral work and worship that is the normal, day-to-day round of the Church.

Most politicians' criticisms of Churches tend to be rather ill-informed and self-serving. They try to do with the Church as they do with other critics and somehow dismiss and undermine the arguments they are uncomfortable with.

What are the values that underpin your moral vision?

As a Liberal, I obviously attach very great importance to the individual and wish to safeguard the individual's rights but also the sense that he or she is part of the community. Freedom depends not just on the maintenance of rights – through a Bill of Rights, freedom of information and things of that kind – but also on working together in a community. Therefore I would want to give individuals power and responsibility to make decisions, along with others, about their lives and the whole community in which they live.

I would want to ensure that the state does those things which need to be done for the health of society and can't be done better by the market or voluntary effort.

I'd want to ensure that we recognise our trusteeship of the earth. My commitment is to a society in which you breathe freely, and don't feel oppressed by tiresome rules and regulations, and yet there are a variety of mechanisms, some of them, maybe, tax-based, to ensure that we don't destroy the freedom of others in subsequent generations by what we do.

There are a lot of important values in the recognition that we are part of a world community and that no responsibility stops at these shores. So I would certainly see Liberal Democrats fighting against the endless preoccupation with sovereignty within the United Kingdom, when so many of the decisions that need to be made are international. It seems extraordinary that you could have an increasing preoccupation with hanging on to national decision-making when everything economic, every technology, is making the world a smaller place.

You certainly can't stop that happening, and if you ignore it, the right decisions will not be made. It's true in environmental matters as well. You may feel terribly pleased with yourself if you've ended some particularly damaging practice in your own country, but what happens in other countries will affect the air and the sea.

So it's much better to embrace it and see what we can do with it. People travel much more now; they see on television what's going on in the rest of the world. We should be welcoming with enthusiasm the opportunities to make a better world.

Even if that means a reduction of fiscal sovereignty?

That is effectively happening through agreements on trade and tariffs. All sorts of international agreements designed to promote free trade, for example, make it impossible for us to operate a tax regime in total defiance and ignorance of what's going on in the rest of the world.

We don't all have to be the same. There's plenty of room for local difference in cultural style and policy. There is plenty of scope for genuine pride in the heritage of your country. I am very happy to fly the Union flag, to see the Guards marching down the Mall. I am a supporter of the monarchy.

But the world is now a much smaller place and the delight we take in our national heritage should not blind us to the fact that we are now a global community.

But globalisation is not all good news, is it? If our labour costs are higher than those of other countries, it may in the long run drive industry to the Pacific Rim.

I'm a free-trader. I believe that of the possible options the best system is the most open system of free trade, which allows parts of the world to develop what they can do best. The alternative drives you further and further into isolation. Your own industries become more and more inefficient, and other countries are deprived of the opportunity of earning their living by selling goods to your people. You deprive your consumers of a better deal. You exclude the goods of other countries. We saw that happen with the countries of Eastern Europe. It happened to such an extent that it's very difficult to unscramble now without a great deal of pain.

There is a moral issue behind the idea of "fair trade". If you impose unrealistic standards on other countries, you effectively keep their goods out of your market. There is an unfortunate coincidence of objective between those who say that if we do that we're helping to raise standards in the Third World and those who say we can stop imports of low-price goods which compete with what we produce. You get hidden protectionism, which actually costs jobs and livelihoods in the Third World.

All the main political parties are now talking about personal responsibility. Does this new emphasis represent a new political agenda because there's a general feeling that we have gone too far in our emphasis on rights?

In some respects, rights have been reduced rather than increased. It's hard to think of many people who have had their rights enlarged or enhanced in a significant way in recent years. There was an emphasis in the Thatcher years on individualism, but it wasn't always associated with rights and the wider distribution of power because in some ways central government became more powerful. Local communities lost rights extensively and haven't regained them.

But it is true, I think, that there is now a greater interest in responsibilities, probably across the political spectrum. We have created a notion of dutiless rights – that you have all sorts of rights but none of them carry any duties with them. We have to deal with it in some way. Does membership of society confer duties on you? I think most people would recognise that it does, but that has not been emphasised very much.

I think that part of the picture is going to be looked at much more, by different parties in different ways. For us, it is fundamental to our whole notion of community. There's a very optimistic Liberal belief that if you give

Alan Beith

people more responsibility, they will come to understand their duty better and behave more responsibly. So you devolve power, to nations and regions and local communities, and let people make their own decisions. It doesn't work in all cases, but it's still better to attempt it. We're very hostile to the centralisation of power.

Conservatives, I think, are using the idea of responsibility as a kind of replacement for various kinds of state provision. Most of them don't think in terms of rights but of what the individual can achieve. They really want to cut back the state while relying on individuals to provide for themselves and assuming that individual effort will also lead to a lot of philanthropy which can fill in the gaps. I think they are now very confused. Mrs Thatcher developed the idea that the activity of the state undermined the moral capacity of the individual by creating dependency, and there is some truth in that, and it is now recognised by people in all parties. But the conclusions she drew from it became increasingly horrific.

By almost general consent, people feel they have gone too far, and so they take this new talk of responsibility ill from the Conservatives. They see the Government taking away basic provision and therefore not setting an example of duty to others. Also, they see it as a Government which doesn't like local power. Some of those on the right who talk of responsibility make it sound very much like a qualification of rights: your rights have to be limited because you have to behave in ways the state wants you to behave.

That is traditionally socialist thinking as well, but there's not much real socialism around these days. Tony Blair has now abandoned so much of socialism that it is difficult to see what his party's basic philosophy is. At the moment, I see Labour as a party which has said that all of its previous solutions either wouldn't work or are not saleable, so all they're offering to do is to manage the country in a slightly more benevolent way than the Conservatives.

What difference does it make when Liberal Democrats come to power?

In Britain, of course, it's qualified by the incredibly restricted position that local authorities are in: there's so little they can do. But one of the first priorities is to try to distribute power more widely, and to try to open up the process to people. So you'll find that councils have opened up meetings so that people can come and petition or present their view direct to the councillors. In many places area committee systems have been developed so that instead of everything being run from a remote town or county hall, people in the locality can get together and contribute much more to decisions. You'll find a desire to improve public services – not the automatic assumption that the local authority can provide the best services but a fairly pragmatic view: how can we achieve the best services economically and sensibly? We have long been interested in partnership with the private sector, but we're not averse to the local authority doing something if nobody else can do it and it's important.

And if the Liberal Democrats formed a national Government, what could we expect?

Strengthening constitutional rights through a Bill of Rights; devolving power to Scotland and Wales and, as shown to be required, the regions of England as well. The whole constitutional package: open government, freedom of information. Along with this notion of extending people's rights comes the belief that if you want people to exercise responsibility, you've got to give them some power to do so. If you minimise that power, the natural inclination will be to blame somebody else for anything that goes wrong. Take local government: the Government has so whittled down the power of local authorities that they can spend their time saying, "Whatever's wrong is the central government's fault because they won't let us raise taxation." That does not encourage taking responsibility for difficult decisions.

As Liberals, we see education as absolutely crucial because it is the means by which people can exercise rights in society. If you don't have education, you are impaired in your ability to get a job, to have economic security, maybe to contribute to making decisions. Education is a very high priority. We're prepared, if necessary, to increase taxation in order to fund it. The Tories have starved it of resources. They have also pushed through endless (and, in many cases, contradictory) changes in curriculum content because they didn't really know what they were doing. They've rushed at things, and therefore they've demoralised teachers and made their life more difficult. Part of what they were doing was right and justified in trying to sharpen up the curriculum and to ensure that children had access to a basic range of skills and knowledge which would equip them for life. That, I think, in principle was right. But they really did make the most appalling mess of it.

And they've shown a certain amount of arrogance too

– believing they'd got the answer and therefore they could order the entire army to march in one particular direction and, a few minutes later, discovering that was wrong, so they marched the entire army in reverse. It is one of the features of majority government under the present system that they can feel they can order people around. And they want to take education, as far as we can see, increasingly out of any kind of local democracy altogether. Many of them, including the Prime Minister, now seem to want every school to be grant-maintained – in other words, to owe its allegiance and funding to a national body. The system as a whole would be entirely directed from the centre.

The Liberal Democrats are the only party contemplating an increase in direct taxation. Are you assuming that people would feel better off if they had better public services than if they paid less taxes?

Of course, taxation is a balance. You have to try to ensure that you don't weaken incentives or consume too large a share of public expenditure for the health of the economy. It's difficult at the moment to be sure what the position will be in, say eighteen months' time, which is why we use the phrase "if necessary". We aren't wedded to high taxation as a matter of principle.

But the Labour Party's got itself stuck in this situation that its members are not allowed to refer to any possibility of increasing taxes whatsoever because they believe they lost the last election over tax. So they've ruled themselves out of promoting a responsible public view of taxation and its stultifying political debate.

Why do you believe in democracy?

I believe it is better than any other form of political organisation at preventing the abuse of power which is inherent in fallen humanity.

But we have a basic conviction that to make a democratic society work, all the groups in it need to be able to feel that their contribution is respected. That is much less likely to happen in a first-past-the-post system, because the whole ethos of the system is for a group to get the majority and then to be given absolute freedom to do what they want until another group can take over.

Proportional representation gives power much more extensively to the various groups that make up a society and makes it much more necessary for the politicians to seek wider consent for what they are trying to do. If there was a majority, it would have to be found – and that would reflect reality because there is not a majority in this country for any one party.

Of course, in local government the Conservatives have actually suffered now from the system they so adore because they have lost council seats disproportionately. In Richmond, we hold nearly every council seat because we have defeated every Conservative candidate in every ward, whereas in fact their votes in the constituency as a whole amount to 35 per cent.

But nationally the Government has unrestricted power to bring in the poll tax, to privatise the entire railway system and other things which most people are against.

The younger generation seems to be disenfranchised from national politics. Generation X is interested only in single-issue politics, if at all. If that continues, the number of people who vote is going to drop persistently.

It's an extremely worrying state of affairs. Even the interest in single-issue politics is quite limited. We do attract young people into our own party, but we need an electoral system in which their effect could be felt, where a young candidate could get backed by large numbers of young people. We'd like to lower the voting age and lower the age at which people can stand for election. They can undertake so many other things at the age of sixteen, why shouldn't people vote at sixteen? Why shouldn't they stand for election for their local council? The British people as a whole can decide whether they have a good contribution to make.

And young people's expectations have changed. There's a whole culture, around the entertainment industry particularly, which positively waits on young people, sees them as consumers, wishes to attract their interest, while the political world, with a few exceptions, seems to take no real interest in them at all and to offer them no hope or excitement.

We are most anxious to bring young people into the process and there are a lot of factors offering some kind of hope. Young people who readily travel round Europe and see things done better in other countries, most of them are not susceptible to the idea that somehow the rest of the world is inhabited by dangerous foreigners and we must have no more to do with them. They are not at all convinced by the idea that the shortages and difficulties they have seen in their own education can be justified

Alan Beith

in order to lower levels of taxation for people who are
well off.

*Are you optimistic about the direction our culture is
taking?*

I am not a deep pessimist. I suppose it's partly a matter
of faith. God has the future in his hands and somehow
new opportunities will develop and new challenges will
be met.

Biography

Alan Beith was born in 1943, the son of a packer. He was
educated at King's School, Macclesfield, and Balliol and
Nuffield Colleges, Oxford.

From 1966 to 1973 he lectured in politics at Newcastle
University. In 1970 he contested Berwick-on-Tweed for
the Liberals, and three years later he won the seat in
a by-election by fifty-seven votes. The two general
elections of 1974 saw his majority rise to 443 before
falling back to seventy-three.

In 1976 he was appointed Chief Whip, a position he
held until 1985, when he became Deputy Leader. He
spoke on treasury affairs between 1987 and 1994 and has
also been his party's spokesperson on education, constitutional and parliamentary affairs and foreign affairs.

He became Deputy Leader of the Liberal Democrats in
1988, after losing to Paddy Ashdown in the leadership
election, and is the party spokesman on police, prisons
and security.

47

He was appointed a Privy Councillor in 1992.

He is a member of the House of Commons Commission, which is responsible for the budget and staffing of the House of Commons, and he answers parliamentary questions on behalf of the Commission. He is also a member of the Intelligence and Security Committee. He is vice-chair of the All-Party Parliamentary Group on Non-Profit-Making Members' Clubs.

Alan Beith is a Methodist local preacher and can speak Norwegian and Welsh. He is married, with one son and one daughter.

Two interviews were conducted on 8 December 1994 and 31 October 1995.

Tony Blair

You identify yourself as a Christian. How did you come to that faith?

I was brought up as a Christian, but I was not in any real sense a practising Christian until I went to Oxford. There was an Australian priest at the same college as me who got me interested in religion again, and, unusually, I became confirmed at university.

In a sense it was a rediscovery of religion as something living, that was about the world around me rather than some sort of special one-to-one relationship with a remote being on high (which is very much the Christianity I had been brought up with). Suddenly I began to see its social relevance. I suppose it coincided with a period of political development for me, and that rediscovery of Christianity as something that can be both exciting, enjoyable and relevant was tremendously important to me. I began to make sense of the world around me.

For a time I almost rebelled against the Church and saw Christianity almost in humanist terms. Now, as I've got older, that has changed, and I would see the two things combining together.

Belief in Politics

How does a socialism based on Christianity differ from one based on Marxism?

Marxism was an economic theory which purported to be almost deterministic in its view of human beings and their development. It came to represent the belief (though I don't think Marx ever really believed this or, in fact, that most thinking Marxists quite believe it) that personal responsibility was swallowed up in social responsibility and that society would determine you as an individual.

I don't think I ever quite believed that. To me, socialism has always been a set of values, not some determinist economic perspective. That is very important because what drove a lot of Christians away from socialism in the end was the belief that somehow you as a person were less important than the state.

Where my political and personal beliefs completely coincide is in the notion that people are members of the community and society, not simply individuals, isolated and alone. (I think the term "community" requires a lot more definition, but it is at least a very useful counterpoint to the alternative, which is a very crude form of individualism. I think that most ordinary people understand the concept of community and understand its importance.)

You are what you are in part because of others, and you cannot divorce the individual from the surrounding society. Indeed, socialism started off as a theory about society, and I think that notion is very clear not just in Christian teaching but in Old Testament teaching as well. That idea of the individual and their place in society is to me (apart from the spiritual dimension) the distinguishing philosophical feature of the Christian religion, and it just happens to be the same as my political belief.

But the notion of the individual within a community is not a substitute for individual responsibility. You have to live your own life and take responsibility for the decisions you make. When I say that Christianity is a tough religion, I think there are certain imperatives of individual conduct that it is very strong on. It is not a religion that makes easy excuses for people. The way I have reinterpreted the socialist message politically is to say that social responsibility is important to reinforce personal responsibility, not as a substitute for it, and I think that is, in the end, what the Christian religion is about.

How do you square the pragmatism of current politics with such a conscience-based approach? Do you have a vision for the future of Britain?

Yes, I do. The task for my political party is to rebuild Britain as a strong community, recognising that individual advancement is only possible within it. And that is a function economically and socially. The notion of public intervention is absolutely essential if we are to put right some of the problems of the country – the appalling social division, the waste of talent and ability through unemployment and lack of access to decent education and training. I think you can articulate a very strong vision.

But people use the word "pragmatic" in two senses. One means that, for simple reasons of expediency, you don't take a course which you believe to be right. The other meaning is just that politics is the art of the possible, and you have to try to take people with you. You have to make sure that your policy does not create problems that are worse than the problems you were trying to cure.

Now, that is pragmatism in a perfectly decent sense, and provided you keep that distinction in mind, you don't go far wrong.

Politicians have been very bad at educating the public – and being honest with the public – about some of the difficult decisions they face. Partly because of the nature of our politics, there is a tendency for those in government not to tell the truth and for those in opposition always to pretend that life could be made so much better so very easily. In fact, of course, it can't. In the end, if politicians spend their time lying to the public, that just devalues politics, and if you devalue politics, you've got a problem.

There are double standards. I remember being asked a question on *Any Questions?* some years ago and deciding I would be completely honest and say, "I haven't the faintest idea what the answer is." Afterwards people said, "You can't go round saying that, for God's sake – they'll think you're not fit to run the country!"

In the end, I'm in politics because political decisions are so important to the things I believe in. The actual business of politics, although I can do it, I don't have a great deal of time for, and if I felt I really couldn't make a difference, I wouldn't much bother. I don't particularly enjoy the trappings of politics – indeed, I dislike a lot of them intensely.

Church leaders have been heavily criticised for the way they have condemned or supported government policy. Do you think that is right?

It would be completely absurd if the Church were silent on the big issues of the day. It's important that the

Church does not become an adjunct of any particular political party, but I think it would be quite bizarre if there were enormous problems in society and the Church said, "Well, look, I'm afraid those aren't for us, those are for the politicians. We'll just talk to you in church every Sunday."

I think there's a lot of good in the Church, actually, and it's had a much worse press than it deserves. On the whole, in a world where there's a lot of bad around, the Church does try to do some good, and we should be thankful for that.

What must Labour do if it is to achieve power?

I really think we have got to face up to social change. The great problem for Labour has been the failure to distinguish between a set of policy perspectives for one generation and a set of principles. The principles of the Labour Party don't change, but the way that they're applied of course has got to change.

I don't think the public really has any interest in the debate between public and private sector. I think it is much more interested in the standard of service. To me, the Labour Party has to show how it will improve public services; simply to say we will renationalise them, and that's how you improve them, does not really count with people any more.

Any system after a time requires revolution and reform, and the welfare state is like any other institution. That is what I keep saying in the Labour Party. Our job is not just to sit there and defend the status quo because that was the 1945 settlement or whatever. Our job is to put sensible reform in place, to improve it in accordance with the original values that gave rise to it.

We have to show how we reach out to those who live in their own homes as well as council tenants, and those who are working in offices and the service sector as well as those in manufacturing. The danger comes when people regard that as leaving principle behind.

The left of your party generally believes that the reason Labour has lost is because it has not been left-wing enough. You obviously don't agree.

It would be curious if the public were voting Tory when what they wanted was a more left-wing Labour Party. People say: "Why do 50 per cent of trade unionists vote Tory? Because Labour is not strong enough in its support of trade unions." Well, there are some highly illogical people in the British electorate if they're voting Tory for that reason.

The truth is that between 1979 and 1983 the left had control of the party organisation and policy, and when we went in on their manifesto in 1983 we almost went out of business. Since then we have come back a long way, but not nearly far enough, and the reason for that is perfectly simple. For thirty years the Labour Party has been debating whether to accept social change and reapply its principles to a changed society, or to carry on in the belief that at some point in time the electorate will change back again. Well, it won't. Harold Wilson managed to skirt round that problem, but it's still there and we've got to resolve it.

Labour always used to talk of equality, rarely of freedom. Is the new emphasis on freedom a necessary accommodation of market capitalism, or is it a matter of principle?

I think it's entirely principled because that is what equality is about – the belief that if people are not equal, then they are less free, less able to develop.

People on the left have made far too little of the fact that the nature of capitalism and market economies has changed dramatically this century as a result of the things our type of government has done. We are way, way behind in our analysis of capitalism as a market because people have thought that the choice is between nineteenth-century capitalism and Marxism, and it's not.

If freedom and equality go hand in glove, doesn't that mean that a principled approach to freedom should mean higher taxes?

Well, it may do. I don't say that the Labour Party should never raise taxes, but if we are to raise taxes or to spend more money, we have got to demonstrate to the public the purposes to which it is to be put. The problem for Labour in the past has been that people thought we would raise tax just for the sake of it.

Bill Clinton's Democrats stopped talking about taxes and started talking about investing and growing. It may come to the same thing, but you start with the proposition that you are not going to tax people just because you are anti-wealth. That is an important part of repositioning Labour.

With regard to law and order you have said much about the relationship between social roots and personal responsibility. Is that, for you, the major theme in the debate?

It's a major theme throughout my belief about what we have to do as a society and how Labour must change. A modern notion of citizenship is about rights and responsibilities: the problem for the right has been that they haven't given people the opportunities and the rights, and the problem for the left has traditionally been that it has underestimated the importance of personal responsibility. What I have tried to do is transcend that argument and say, "Look, in fact what you want is to combine the two."

The sensible thing is to give young people a stake in our society: to give them respect but demand respect in return. You don't have to choose between old-style ideas. The left had allowed itself to be put in a position where it basically never said, "This person has done something wrong and has got to go inside." I think that was an important shift for us to make.

To what extent would you attribute the rise of violence in our society to a decline in personal morality? And what has caused that decline?

In part these things are a natural development as societies become more prosperous, as all the means of communication – television and so on – develop. I don't mean that violence is an expression of envy. But as society reaches a level of prosperity – people own cars, videos, all the rest of it – you've got young people with a lot more money to spend. They go to pubs, they drink, they can travel around much more easily, and I think that strong community values tend to break down. In some ways this problem is bound to appear at a certain level of development in society.

However, I think that notions of personal responsibility, of mutual obligation within society, are very, very important. What has happened is that as strong community and family ties have broken down, so all the normal mechanisms of reinforcement for personal responsibility and obligation have not disintegrated – that's too strong a word – but certainly declined.

In a curious way, I think the Labour Party message is actually more relevant today than ever. We have to find ways to re-encapsulate proper community and family values. It's all the more important because they're not being reinforced by circumstances.

I think you can see this very clearly in the old mining villages in my constituency. There used to be very strong community ties, but they aren't there any more. We need to rebuild them, otherwise you will find there is an element of society which grows up outside the mainstream, which has no stake in it, which sees how the rest of the world lives and is pretty antagonistic towards it.

But aren't you ignoring the fact that community and family values are expressions of a fundamentally religious outlook which we have lost? Isn't the root cause of the fragmentation of our society and the rise in violence the spread of secularism?

Well, I think it is certainly to do with the absence of

strong moral, philosophical and spiritual values. There are economic factors as well that reinforce that – if you've got very high levels of youth unemployment, and young people feel they just can't make any headway.

There was a tendency at one time to think that people could live in a spiritual and moral vacuum, that you could simply stop teaching these types of values and people would make their own way towards their accommodation with society. There were elements of Utopia in that: the belief that you can create some sort of perfect society in which people naturally gravitate towards these values. I think we have a slightly more hard-headed understanding now that these values have to be taught and learned. You can see, as a father bringing up your children, it is a constant problem: they don't just get to it by themselves.

But you could argue for change on the basis of enlightened self-interest as well as on the basis of community values. If you start atomising society and just exist as individuals, economically and socially, you end up with the problem we've got. We live in a society with an individuated culture and lifestyle. Where you try to advocate and persuade is to say, "Look, if you take that very narrow view of self-interest, we don't end up with a better society and you don't end up with greater individual prosperity."

People are very cynical about political leadership now. What do you think are the qualities of leadership that this country needs?

First of all, to tell people how the world really is. Secondly, I think, to be less tribal in our outlook as party politicians. And, as much as anything else, to give people some sense of hope that change is possible and that it's not something to be frightened of.

Biography

Tony Blair was born in Edinburgh in 1953 and educated at Durham Choristers' School and Fettes College. He went on to study law at St John's College, Oxford.

He was called to the Bar in 1976 and served his pupillage with the Labour grandee, Lord Irvine, QC, in whose offices he met his fellow pupil and future wife, Cherie Booth.

He contested the safe Conservative seat of Beaconsfield in a by-election in 1982 and was elected MP for Sedgefield in County Durham a year later.

In 1984 he was appointed Opposition spokesperson on treasury and economic affairs and, in 1986, deputy spokesperson for trade and industry, with special responsibility for consumer affairs and city issues.

He was elected to the Shadow Cabinet in 1988, taking first the portfolio for energy for a year and then for employment until 1992, when he became shadow Home Secretary.

In 1994, following the death of John Smith, he was elected leader of the Labour Party, beating John Prescott and Margaret Beckett.

This interview was conducted on 14 September 1993.

Paul Boateng

What is your background?

I was born in Hackney, of mixed African and British parents. When I was three, we went to Ghana, where I was brought up. My father was a barrister and then a Cabinet minister, my mother a teacher. It was a time of great change; Ghana was the first independent black African country and a centre of Third World politics. There was a constant stream of political personalities from all over the world through Ghana and, to a certain extent, our own front room. It was an exciting time for a young boy to grow up in.

My family knew the dangers of politics: the way you could be up one moment and down the next. My father sometimes returned from the northern territories with bullet holes in the car. I remember, as a little boy, asking him about them. Ultimately he was arrested and flung into prison without trial, and we had to flee the country as refugees.

We were fortunate to have had a strong Christian upbringing to keep us stable throughout all that. Faith was very much part of one's life. Church was a very happy, joyful experience.

Paul Boateng

What were the values it instilled in you?

Values of involvement, of caring, of community and respect. I think the central value was the notion that Christian duty and civic duty are entwined. You just could not be other than involved in society. You couldn't not care about what was happening, not only to the people around you but to the environment as well.

One of my earliest memories is of De Gaulle testing the atom bomb in the Sahara. So I grew up knowing that the *hamatan*, the wind that blows from the north, was potentially contaminated. Ghana is an incredibly luxuriant country, and in a sense one was brought up to see nature and its produce as something we had to treasure as Christians.

Was it always inevitable that you would make a career in politics?

No. I am a lawyer. I have never seen politics as a career, politics is a vocation. I see it very much as a form of service, an opportunity, at a particular time in one's life, to make a contribution.

Who knows what the future holds? I have no illusions about a political life, and I don't worry much about what it holds for me personally. What I do worry about, desperately, is whether or not we will have a Labour Government. I believe we will. What role I may play in it I honestly don't know, but I do know that I intend to take advantage of every opportunity I have, so long as I live, to do the best I can and make a contribution. That's how one has been brought up and that's the basis

61

of one's life as a Christian. You work hard, you enjoy the wonders of God's creation and you play your part in it.

Given the amount of pressure politicians live with, how do you find room for personal prayer and the stillness it takes, in a sense, to be in touch with God?

I don't think the opportunity to pray and to reflect is any more crowded out by a political life than it is by stacking shelves in Tesco or having to work down a mine or being a teacher and coming home at night (as I've seen my mother do) absolutely exhausted from giving her all to children throughout the day. Sure, it's a stressful life, but all the more reason to find time for quiet, for communicating with God and seeking a space for the Spirit in your life. There is a real need, in my view, if you are leading a political life, to have a sense of proportion and a grounding. The wonderful thing about a belief in the power of the Holy Spirit and in God's love for us and for the world is that it gives you that grounding.

To what extent are your political convictions based on your reading of the Bible or do you keep your faith and your politics separate?

No. It's one life which we have to seek to make whole, which does not mean there are not enormous contradictions, and of course there are tensions in one's own life. But at least in the love of God there is the possibility, on this earth and certainly in the hereafter, of wholeness and oneness.

But the Bible is not some sort of manifesto, and I have very grave reservations about the use of scripture, either by church people or by politicians, to authenticate their own ideology or political perspective. For me, it transcends ologies and isms: the thing about the spiritual life is that without it these are ultimately empty and futile. What the Bible does, it seems to me, is to ground very firmly the view that any political system based on the belief that it is possible to attain happiness and fulfilment through material things alone is ultimately doomed to fail. This for me has always been the weakness of both Marxism and capitalism.

I look to the Gospels to provide a bedrock of faith and values on which it is possible to build an agenda for this world. We certainly find much in the Bible that speaks to us of this age; I completely reject the notion that it has nothing to say to us, for instance, about the economy. It has a great deal to say, if you look at Isaiah and Amos – the references there to selling the poor for a pair of shoes, to excessive interest rates, to waste and disrespect for the environment.

Does the Church then have a distinctive contribution to make to political life?

Of course it has. Our faith is, in its way, profoundly subversive. Any faith that takes the cross, an instrument of torture, as St Paul says, "for the Jews an abomination, for the Greeks foolishness", and turns it into a vehicle for liberation has got something very challenging to say to people like myself who occupy places supposedly of power. It is for the Church to challenge the prevailing political wisdom of the time.

I don't think it is doing it very effectively. Let me give you an example. It doesn't hesitate to talk about the redistribution of wealth and our responsibilities in that regard. It is actually quite good at that. But it is very bad at talking about the creation of wealth. It is terrified in case it gets its hands dirty. There was a time when it was very much engaged in the world of work and had something to say to challenge the prevailing mood of industry and commerce, not simply in terms of social responsibility but as to the purposes of economic growth and systems in the context of creation.

You refer to tensions in your own life between your faith and your politics. What have been the greatest?

If you are a politician, time and time again the pressures are to deliver *now*. If you are a Christian, you have a different timescale, and there is a constant tension there which you have to seek to resolve. A week may be a long time in politics but in the context of eternity a decade is as nothing.

There is also the continuing vexed issue of suffering and God's purposes. I have to contemplate the fact that the past seventeen monstrous years may have been for a reason, when to me as a politician they just seem to have been the most appalling waste and the cause of the most enormous suffering, which I see weekly in my surgeries, getting worse and worse and worse. But I have to face the fact that maybe it wasn't a waste, that maybe it was part of a wider purpose whose meaning is not clear to me. Humility is always a challenge to politicians.

Your constituency is one of the poorest in the country.

It's one of the most economically deprived. I make the distinction because if you were to compare the spiritual life of my community, and I'm not thinking simply of the Christian faith, with that of some of the economically most privileged places in the Home Counties, I can assure you that you would see very clearly where the poverty is. Very clearly. Our churches are packed. We build new churches and temples while they are shutting theirs down and turning them into stripped-pine shops.

I do see terrible economic and social deprivation. I see gross overcrowding: a couple and five children in two rooms. I see an appalling waste of talent, as a light-manufacturing base is destroyed and we are lucky to get warehouses in its place. I see young people who are not getting the chances they ought to be getting because of the pressure on resources in schools. Increasingly, I see old people eking out an existence, with enormous problems in paying for gas and electricity, for whom the VAT was the last straw. Also I see the opportunities that people ought to have to make a contribution to their communities in local government valued less and less by central government, a more authoritarian and centralised regime than was ever the case.

Belief in Politics

Does that fill you with despair or with resolution?

St Augustine said that hope has two beautiful daughters: anger at what is and determination to do something about it. I think that's very much the case for me, and I'm sure I'm not alone in my party in experiencing that.

At times, when you're just exhausted and empty, you're not very nice to be around. I go home to my wife and kids after surgeries, and unless I'm very careful I tend to be irritable and difficult. One of the ways in which we have coped with that as a family is that from time to time the children come with me. It makes them aware of what Daddy does; they see why Daddy goes off to meetings and why he comes home late at night. And it makes me aware of them and my responsibility to them not to let it get me down. Also many of my constituents bring their children with them, because they've got no one else to look after them, and they know that one or more of mine will be there too.

What, for you, are the burning economic, social or moral issues that face our country?

There is development and the global environment: my experience is that young people are very much aware of what is happening to that and to other species, and I think we need to relate to that. It would be sad if we were to concentrate solely on the domestic issues.

Employment is a burning domestic issue, in which I would include education, the acquisition of skills and training, and the challenge of structuring society in a way that enables people to have a sense of their own

66

worth through their work. Even if they are not going to
be working all their lives, they should have opportunities
to contribute.

Housing is a very important area, which we have
neglected most shamefully as a society. We do not
look at the issue of homelessness, of overcrowding, of
bad housing that *contributes* to poor health. The asthma
and the lung infections, the depression and mental illness
in my constituency have a direct link to poor housing
– there's no doubt about that in my mind whatsoever.
Yet the only headlines we see relate to mortgage interest rates.

Similarly, what's happening to communities and families is linked to housing. If you've got no chance of
having your elderly mother or father live anywhere near
you, if you have to move and split families apart, or if
you have to keep families together when they ought not
to be living together, then we pay a price. Our families
are splintered and alienated; it's very difficult for them
to be anything else.

*Is bad housing the only reason for the fragmentation of
our society? What about the emphasis on individualism
which in the last ten years especially has been fed by the
entertainment industry, say, and by consumerism?*

Yes, but it's no use crying out against the values of the
entertainment industry unless one is addressing what
actually lies at the heart of our problems. And that
is not what's in the Top Ten at any particular time,
whether Snoop Doggy Dog does represent the proper
approach to relationships. Of course you don't want

to bring children up to believe that women should be referred to as "bitches" or "whores". You don't want to bring them up to denigrate people because of their sexuality or whatever. But those manifestations of popular culture, and our television and our newspapers, simply reflect the deep-rooted problems that exist within our society. They're not a cause of it. I think we have to get this in perspective.

I do think it's possible for public taste to be degraded by a mass-communication industry that caters to the lowest common denominator, yes. But I don't believe we should spend our time railing against the messenger. We have to address the source of the message. It's too easy for Christians to believe that they are fulfilling their Christian responsibility by writing a letter to the BBC or Sony or Rupert Murdoch or whoever. All too often that's an excuse for not doing anything about the causes.

If people wish to do it, then that's a matter for them; I'm not condemning them. I just don't think that's the answer. I don't believe, for instance, that the activities of Mary Whitehouse contributed one iota towards arresting the decline in standards in broadcasting. On the contrary. What would arrest the decline is bringing children up to have discerning taste. If people are only educated to a level at which they can just about read the *Sun*, then large numbers of them will read it.

Though it doesn't do to get too snobbish about the *Sun*, it must be said. If you look in any university common room you will see large quantities of the *Sun* next to the coffee cups and the beer mugs. But if, as I do, you want people to be turned on by great literature and great music rather than simply by *Neighbours* and some of the less edifying aspects of popular culture,

you must give them the wherewithal to respond to the
alternatives.

*Shouldn't the Labour Party be committed to full
employment?*

If you mean by full employment the opportunity to work
and to lead a worthwhile and gainful life, of course. If
you mean everybody having a job always, then that may
no longer be an attainable goal. The global economy
has changed. There have been massive advances in
technology, and fundamental changes in patterns of
industrial production.

And I don't believe that there's necessarily anything
particularly improving about lifelong, boring, degrading
– as it can be – mindless toil. There was full employment
in the time of slavery. When children worked from the
age of ten until their lives ended at forty-five, they were
fully employed. What I want people to be able to do is
to develop their talents to a maximum and for them to be
occupied and for us as a society to be sufficiently caring
for that to be possible, as it should be.

*Aren't employment levels now dictated by the global
economy? There isn't much that governments can do
about them.*

There is no doubt in my mind that one of the reasons
we need to be full, active and central members of
the European Community is precisely because national
governments have only limited scope to directly affect

economic conditions within their territory. That's one of the reasons why we need to construct a model for global trade and cooperation. And Christians need to be proclaiming that such models must be just and in keeping with the integrity of Creation.

The limited sovereignty of national government is an economic fact of life. I don't see how it can be denied. That's why global cooperation is no longer a matter that can be left simply to idealists. It should not be seen as a vague, unattainable idea. We've got to make it practical politics.

Labour are sounding more and more like the Conservatives: you even insist that you don't want to raise taxes. Does this mean that Labour is no longer a truly radical party?

I am a radical. So is Tony Blair and those around him. It is because we are a radical party that we are now attracting the numbers of people that we are, because the Labour Party is the party best equipped to take this country into the next century unencumbered by some of the baggage that it and the political process as a whole have accumulated over the years. Radicalism is about a willingness to apply intellectual discipline and rigour to the solution of present problems, unafraid of the challenges that this may bring to existing beliefs and practices. It is a mistake to confuse radical solutions with high-spending ones.

We are certainly not in the business of putting taxes up. One of the causes of hardship among people in my constituency has been the increase in their taxes, so the last thing I want to do is to put tax up. I want us to cut taxes for people on low and middle incomes. I want us to be able to satisfy the voter that we mean to make the most of the resources we have and to be serious about the business of generating wealth. Because only when you have accepted the challenge of the creation of wealth can you get to a position in which you can make sure that that wealth is applied in ways that are beneficial to the community as a whole. The economic challenge of this age is the sustainable creation of wealth, sustainable in terms of the environment and social cohesion, without the stop-go, stop-go situation that has bedevilled the post-war economy. We must avoid the social disintegration that is the inevitable result of making unyielding, unrestrained or unregulated market forces a Moloch, a tin god, devouring its own creation.

But surely the electorate realises that more money has to be spent on education and the social services, and that can only be done if there is an increase in taxation?

It is naive to believe that the problems of the welfare state or of education or, indeed, of housing are to be addressed solely by spending more money. Of course, we want to see resources applied in the most cost-efficient way possible. But haven't we also got to face up to the fact that we have a crisis of attitude and philosophy? Take housing, for instance. There are many societies in which people move from rental to owner-occupation to shared equity to shared homes at different times of their lives and do so with a considerably greater degree of flexibility than we do.

Our obsession, our fetish, with owner-occupancy hasn't

served this country well either in terms of housing policy or in terms of its economic development. Look at the amount of investment potential we've got tied up in bricks and mortar, now burdened by negative equity. So the way forward is actually to begin to approach housing in a rather different way. Christians need to address what the theological basis of ownership and of our relationship with the land ought to be. Some exciting work has been done on this, in South Africa in particular and also among Native Americans. We are obsessed by ownership.

Or take the issue of welfare. Are we satisfied with the way the welfare state is currently constructed? I'm not. I think there are aspects of the system at the moment which stink, and which need to be radically rethought. The notion of welfare simply as a safety net, rather than something which lifts people up and puts them on their feet again, is positively damaging. It destroys personal initiative and undermines a sense of individual responsibility for our neighbours.

So we need a new construct for the welfare state. Who's doing the new and original thinking? Not the Tories. They simply cut it back and go on about scroungers and refugees. That's their approach. The people that are making the really hard contributions to policy are Labour, with the Social Justice Commission first and the subsequent Policy Review.

Many political thinkers are talking of a new politics of responsibilities as well as rights.

For Christians, the very heart of our faith is the notion that duty and responsibility are central to our humanity, what makes human beings special and distinct from the rest of God's Creation. The life of the prophets and of Jesus Christ bears that out.

This notion that we are owed everything as a right is very much a product of the post-war Me generation. And it isn't shared by two-thirds of the globe. My parents' generation, whether here or in Africa, certainly didn't forget that you had to work very hard and you had to accept responsibility for your family and the community of which you were a part. I was brought up in a society in which no one believed anything was owed them. All the people I went to school with believed that education was the way forward and the way out. That's what my parents believed, and that's what I believe. Education, hard work and self-improvement are not to be despised or sneered at but respected and valued.

You are the most prominent black person in the Palace of Westminster, yet you always insist that you are an MP who is black, not a black MP. What does that distinction mean in political life?

If you are black and you are in politics, you do have certain responsibilities. Our sexuality, our race, the extent of our ability or disability, our gender, those are all important things that we obviously can't dispense with, and they do impose certain responsibilities on us. But I believe that my first responsibility as a black person in politics is not to allow the colour of my skin to define me as a politician, any more than it should define me as a person. My black constituents don't want me to say I speak for blacks, they want me to speak for Brent South.

I have never allowed myself the luxury, or accepted the confines, of speaking first and foremost as a black man. I have been true to what I was brought up to believe, that first and foremost I am me, a member of the human race made by God in his image, and that is an image that does not accept the confines of race or gender or sexuality. And my responsibility is to my fellow members of that much wider, global community. Anything else is a cop-out and a self-indulgence. Whether it's an explanation as to one's own success or failure or a reason for taking a particular position on an issue of the day, the question of race, mine or anyone else's, should not be the determining factor of our responses or our sole defining characteristic.

Do you then reject the idea of "political correctness"?

I certainly don't agonise over whether my coffee is black or without milk. I never use the term "political correctness" myself because it is used by people who are opposed to equal rights for blacks, for women, for disabled people and for gays to denigrate positive action to further any cause they do not approve of.

If you ask me if I think we should construct society and its norms around people's race or gender or sexuality or degree of physical ability, I say, "No." If you ask me if it should be illegal to discriminate against people on those grounds, I say, "Yes," because it's a denial of people's humanity and wholeness. Racism is an affront to Christ.

The fact that somebody's black or disabled or gay or a woman is a morally neutral fact; we have no choice in the matter. It does not matter to God that they are, so why should it matter to us? It's neither here nor there in terms of their worth. We are all God's children: each one of us is entitled to that respect and bears that responsibility.

But I continue to hear negative things said about women, about disabled people, about blacks and gays. This remains a constant feature of life. There are still deep-rooted patterns of discrimination on the basis of race and gender. Gay people have no specific legal remedy at all for discrimination against them. That's a failure. And the Disability Discrimination Bill is an apology for a Bill. It isn't what the disabled people in my constituency are calling for, nor what we should want for them as God's children.

We have to fashion a society that counteracts that negativity, that has positive images and that instils and encourages positive values. Is that "political correctness"? I think not. I don't believe it has anything to do with politics. It has everything to do with what the Bible calls righteousness. We have to be prepared to stand up for that, whatever the prevailing mood of the time. As the old spiritual says:

> Dare to be a Daniel,
> Dare to stand alone.
> Dare to have a purpose,
> Dare to make it known.

Biography

Paul Boateng was born in Hackney, London, in 1951, and has been a member of the Labour Party since the age of fifteen. Between the ages of four and fifteen he lived in Ghana, where his father was an MP and a Cabinet minister. He was educated at Apsley Grammar School and at Bristol University, where he graduated with a degree in law.

Between 1975 and 1989, he practised as a solicitor. He is now a barrister and a member of Gray's Inn.

From 1981 to 1986, he was a member of the Greater London Council.

In the general election of 1983 he contested the Conservative-held seat of West Hertfordshire. In the general election of 1987 he ran successfully for the safe Labour seat of Brent South, which he still holds.

He is the first ever British MP of African descent and one of only six non-white MPs in the House of Commons.

He has served on the Select Committee on the Environment and in 1989 was appointed to the Labour front bench as a member of the shadow Treasury team. In 1992 he was appointed to his current front bench position as spokesperson on legal affairs.

He is a Methodist local preacher and a former vice-moderator of the World Council of Churches' programme to combat racism. He is a prolific broadcaster and has written and presented his own television and radio programmes, including *The Black Churches* and *The Christian Faith in Action*. He hosts a Radio 4 chat show entitled *Looking Forward to the Past*. With John Smith, he contributed a chapter to the book *Reclaiming the Ground* (1993).

He is married to Janet, a former social worker and borough councillor, and they have five children.

This interview was conducted on 31 October 1995.

Alistair Burt

How would you describe your upbringing?

Very loving and secure – a good, solid family, great fun. As far as I was aware there were no family difficulties or problems. My dad is recently retired after forty-one years as a GP in Bury. My mum was at home most of the time, helping to run the practice. Religion was always just there. My father in particular has a very strong faith.

I was at the one school from five until eighteen, and that, too, was a very secure environment. I went on to be head of house, captain of cross-country, head boy, all that sort of thing.

After I was confirmed at thirteen, I remember a strong feeling that something had changed. I had a growing belief that I had been very fortunate in the advantages I had been given, and developed a strong sense of responsibility. What could I do with all this? I saw my father giving Christian expression to his life in the work he did in the community, and I found that very moving – and still do.

I wanted to use my skills in a practical way, like my dad, to help people. I couldn't be a doctor because I couldn't stand the sight of blood, and I couldn't do science. So I went to university and read law, but I

never got quite the same spark out of it that I got out
of economics and politics at school.

*Security is obviously important to you. Isn't politics a
strange profession for you to end up in, given both the
conflict and the uncertainty it involves?*

The crucial thing is that security is very strongly linked
to faith. I love what I do. Conflict isn't a difficulty for
me. The fact that I will be argued against and shouted at
is of no concern because I have a job to do and I'm doing
it to the best of my ability. I have confidence that God is
not asking me any questions in life that I can't answer.

I am also confident that while I'm doing this job, both
as minister and as Member of Parliament, this is the right
place for me to be. But if that should ever change, then
there is something else for me to do. I have no worries
whatsoever about what the future will bring, absolutely
none. It's a tremendous feeling with which to go into an
election. Every election I have faced up to now, I have
faced the result with total equanimity.

*Does it disturb you to find other Christians in the
opposition parties?*

Probably my two closest Christian friends in Westminster
are Peter Pike and Simon Hughes. We would disagree as to how we tackle a problem like unemployment, but I wouldn't query their motives for a second
– nor, I suspect, would they query mine. The sense

that we want to do something about it is strong for all of us.

I believe that politics and public life are a calling, but the choice of political parties is pretty secular. Christians can be in any party – that's my choice, not God's. He wants us to be in different parties. I've always believed that if God's world is to work, then his people are to be everywhere. It's also a fundamental for me that he makes us different. The manner in which we argue with one another, I think, is very important, but that sense that we're all involved in God's work has always been very strong.

I don't believe that any one party or political vision is more Christian than any other, and I think it's wrong for any party to claim to be, or for people in the Church to suggest that if you vote for somebody else, your Christianity can be questioned. I do not believe God puts his finger on particular politicians and parties and says, "This is the true way," because we're all flawed.

It's still true, though, that your vision of society differs from that of, say, Peter Pike or Simon Hughes, and yet you would all claim that your politics is influenced by your Christian faith. Are you reading your Bible in the light of your politics, or doing politics in the light of the Bible?

Where Simon's vision and Peter's may go I don't know, but in the essentials, in the development of individuals and society, I think there is a lot that we share. I think the parties of the United Kingdom hold a great deal in common about the structure of our society – even more so now that I find my vision of society and Mr Blair's don't appear to be hugely different – though politics emphasises what differences there are and, crucially, how we would achieve that vision.

I believe that my faith is compatible with Conservative political philosophy because I see Christ's influence in all of us as developing all our potential as human beings. I therefore believe and support a political philosophy that will allow that to emerge. Where all political philosophies run aground is human nature. The collective nature of socialism may be wonderful in theory, but it can become tainted by totalitarianism, by the closed shop, by the economic system we saw in Eastern Europe. A free-market system can become tainted by greed and selfishness and over-concentration on the individual.

I don't believe my party stands for either of those extremes. Virtually every Conservative I know is involved in voluntary activity of one sort or another in their local community, so I reject the idea that Conservatives live in tiny little islands, looking after their own and no one else. That isn't my Conservatism; I don't think it's anybody's that I know.

I don't seek constantly to express the Bible in my politics. I believe my reading of it gives me personal instruction about how I should live my life and what I should do. I believe it also tells me about the society I should work for, and the things I should watch for. There might be certain things I was asked to do or support, or attitudes I might be expected to take, that I could not.

Take salaries, for instance. I was the first minister to express an opinion from the despatch box about an options deal in the water industry, I think. I said that personally I thought it was wrong and I was uncomfortable with it. As a Conservative, I really don't believe you can regulate everyone's salary, but certain things about extremely high salaries in particular situations strike me as not right, and I believe the Bible backs up that sense of injustice.

But, clearly, in a society like ours it's very difficult to generalise. There is a world of difference between the individual who gets money for old rope and the individual who, for the same salary, works immensely hard and produces benefits for all sorts of other people, just as there is a difference between the poor and marginalised, who have had absolutely no opportunity to do anything about their circumstances, and the deliberate wastrel. I think there must be judgments between them, because the Bible is about that.

You repudiate the idea that one party is good and another is evil, but Christianity is not only about morality but also about wisdom. Can you say that your party is wise about what is right for society and other parties are not?

Since 1979 I think the Government has made wiser choices for society than its opponents might have done, a judgment backed by the electorate. However, there will be times when I will consider a policy choice made by my Government and my party to be less wise than one I might hold to. That's bound to happen in a collective group. As a member of the Government, you are bound by what your colleagues decide to do, and in the vast majority of cases, clearly, I am perfectly content. But nobody is 100 per cent happy with every single policy of their party, and it's foolish to believe that. And, let's be honest, there are times when my colleagues are proved right and I am wrong.

As a Christian individual I am responsible for what I do and what I have the ability to influence. In government, though, I have not been involved personally in every decision and am not therefore personally responsible for each decision, I am collectively bound by the actions of my colleagues and rightly so.

Do you feel that sometimes people have impossible expectations of you as a Christian in the Government?

I think there is a low level of understanding of the way government works. It's often suggested that your whole life is a battle between your conscience and the Whips, but it's much more complex than that.

I don't believe you can have 651 individual MPs running around making individual decisions. People come together with a common mind to do a variety of things. There will be times they agree among themselves, and times they disagree, but that's the way decisions are made. If the only things you're prepared to support are decisions with which you agree, you have no structure for running anything beyond a dictatorship. When was the last time everyone on the PCC was unanimous on an issue?

Alistair Burt

Would you agree that many of the most important issues facing society are increasingly out of the reach of politics?

There are real limitations now on the power and influence of politicians. I have long believed that and long had experience of it. Take the economy: within the lifetime of many people, the influence of domestic politicians was much greater than it is now. The bloke wearing a rosette could appear on your doorstep at a general election and you would ask him, in effect, "If I vote for you, am I going to have a job?" and you would expect him to say, "Yes. Vote for me and I'll see that you're safe."

No candidate of any integrity could offer that response today because whether or not someone has a job no longer depends on a politician. International trade and new technology have changed the face of work completely, all over the world. It would not matter which party had been in office, this revolution in work would have happened anyway.

Nor can we alone dictate the quality of law and order in the United Kingdom. Every MP I know, bar none, wants to see a situation in which we are all safer, but we do not believe that on our own we can make that difference. I will support legislation that toughens the criminal law and ensures that the courts have proper sanctions available to them, but I know that does not itself determine the level of crime.

People say, "What are you doing about it? You're an MP." But I can't deliver without their help – no MP can. That's one of the reasons why people have become disappointed in us, perhaps, because we've set ourselves up as able to do things we can't do – or people have the impression that we used to have an influence on these things and now we seem not to. It's much easier for people to blame an identifiable group of people than it is to look at a complex modern society and try to work out what is at fault.

Isn't this Government partly to blame? You have, after all, been promoting the idea of freedom of choice for the last seventeen years.

But freedom of choice doesn't mean that people have to make the wrong choice. I don't see that the world changed radically after 1979 simply because of the Conservative Government. We've been in office for that period, and we have influence, certainly. Some things will never be the same again, that's true. But the general drift of society has been moved by a whole series of other forces as well. Some of those forces I do not like. I feel threatened and frustrated by them because, as an individual and as a politician, I cannot single-handedly turn things round, though I wish I could. I can only work with others to say, "I do not believe this is the right way for society."

You have a great responsibility, when you're putting policy forward, to believe that it's right and proper. For instance, it would be easy for a party to win an election if it offered people what everybody wants. But there are some things, clearly, that might look very attractive but are not right: they would lead your country into danger some way down the line. So politicians have to work with that sense of restraint. We can't give people all they want all the time.

Alistair Burt

But many of the areas of real choice in society are outside politicians' control.

Does someone stay with their family or leave them? No politician is going to dictate that. That's a moral decision to be made which contributes much more to an individual's happiness, and to their family's, than any law that's going to be passed.

Ultimately, if this is to be a free society, people must choose of their own free will what is the right course. The corollaries of freedom have got to be responsibility and duty. Politicians want to aim for a society in which people instinctively make the right choices. That's what we are all working towards.

Would it have been more helpful if the Church commented on a wider range of issues than it has done?

Because present-day politics revolves so much around economic matters, I think there has been an over-concentration on that, and sometimes the contribution of the Church has been very simplistic. That has caused problems. There is sometimes a tendency for some Christians to rail against Conservatives in general. I think the many Conservative Christians who fill the pews find this upsetting and deeply hurtful. If the bloke in the pulpit rails against them as Christians and Conservatives, they won't necessarily question his political wisdom, because they will just think he's wrong, but they will say, "Does this tell me anything about the man's faith?"

That's my concern. If people pick up those sorts of doubts, it might affect their feeling about the rest of

85

what the Church is saying. I think there's plenty of evidence of that.

I think the Church is entitled to comment on the range of matters that it does, and I don't mind it taking a strong view – it's nice to know that it has one. I have never objected to the Church being involved in politics, so long as it has known that it is stepping into our world and deserves a brickbat when it gets it wrong as well as a bouquet when it gets it right.

But the Church's essential message is more important than that. What gives it its moral authority to pronounce on law and order and other matters is the message of Jesus Christ. If that isn't there, then I've got enough people lobbying and marching: another group makes no difference. The Church is different, but it's got to remember why it's different.

Also I wish it would get more prominence for the many things it says in a variety of moral areas which just don't interest the press because they don't suit their book. I think the development of the media in the last twenty years has been potentially hazardous. I know from a conversation I had with the Archbishop of Canterbury not too long ago that of all the sermons and the press releases he produces, nine out of ten go unnoticed by the general press – but all he has to do is put in a sentence suggesting criticism of government policy and it's all over the front pages. I really think that's a disgrace.

The difficulty is to get any issue discussed at any depth in the media today. Media people believe that the general public has a twenty-second attention span, and if things can't be said in that time, they're not worth saying. That's terrible. This is a complex society: I don't think the issues have ever been more difficult for government. Therefore the need for the population to understand and weigh things has never been greater. Anything that raises politics above the tabloid level is welcome in my eyes.

We are often told that the family is breaking up and we are losing our sense of community. How do you account for that if it's true?

One thing, strangely, is communication. Fifty years ago everybody listened to exactly the same thing because the choice was so limited. We had a common culture based on the Light Programme and the Home Service. To an extent, the culture was based on something that everybody knew, so it was much easier to convey a common set of values.

The impact of the communications revolution has been astonishing. It is also linked with changes in attitude in the Fifties and Sixties which focused on the importance of fulfilling yourself. Your first obligation was to be happy yourself. The expansion of information gave people the justification that, whatever they felt, somebody somewhere was going to back them up and say it was right for them to have those feelings. I think that sort of change in the common value system, which occurred long before 1979, has had a profound effect upon us all.

The structure of the family is changing, of that there is no doubt. The statistics tell us, for example, that we have more single-person households and more children growing up without fathers. I think the reasons are many and huge. There must be some blame attached to the Me generation (I'm sorry to use the cliché, but I think it expresses something). Duty and such matters used to be emphasised in personal relationships, which often limited personal freedom, but the changes brought about, in so many different ways, by technological advances in the Fifties and Sixties gave people the opportunity to say, for example, "If I'm feeling good about myself, I'm likely to be a better person for those around me. Therefore if I'm in a relationship which is difficult, the best thing to do is end it. As far as the children are concerned, they will be happier because their parents will be. The divorce will not cause them any pain."

It is one of the classic adult get-outs of our generation. I think it's fundamentally flawed. People want to increase their personal fulfilment and believe they are doing the right thing for those around them.

I am not in any way suggesting that when people enter into relationships they don't matter to them. They do. But the fact is, we have set up a society in which break-up has become easier, and although individual break-ups will always be accompanied by pain, they still happen and they happen a lot.

I think there is a greater acceptance of changing roles in society, of children leaving home early, of couples breaking up. There is a relaxed attitude to all this because people haven't seen the harm that's been done. The harm that divorce and separation do is an unpopular topic, particularly as those who might comment about it often have been through it and may not wish to confront the difficulties it creates. The leaders of the Church, and opinion-formers everywhere, have not risen to the challenge – and it's difficult for politicians to talk about marriage because we are all flawed.

Alistair Burt

Is it not difficult in a pluralist society for anyone to stand against the stream? Cultural relativism has become so dominant in our society that if you object to my lifestyle, all I have to say is: "That's your opinion."

I don't believe all values are relative. I don't believe that on every single subject your view is as good as mine.

I don't mind being judgmental, though I ought to be able to couch my arguments in a way that people don't find offensive: "This is something to aspire to: if your relationships haven't matched up to this, don't worry, but here is something to aim at." That is surely the gentle way to do it, where you're leading rather than condemning.

There must be occasions when you have to say things are right and wrong. I believe the Bible gives you that authority. Moses didn't lay down the Ten Reasonably Acceptable Propositions for Our Time. Jesus's Sermon on the Mount is not a relative manifesto. We've got to believe there are absolutes. Politicians who believe everything is relative and aren't prepared to be judgmental aren't leaders, and you have to lead.

Anyone who's prepared to stand up against the crowd, from the right or left, deserves respect. You see whether they're right or wrong, but the fact that somebody's prepared to challenge is always worth looking at.

In terms of the family, I don't think people have stuck up enough for absolutes. A recognition that we're all flawed is important. You don't want to condemn people, and you must be realistic about marriage and what it can mean not only for the people involved – and the people most involved are the children – but also the extended network around a family. The Church and other opinion-formers in society have tended not to take a stand on this because of fear of standing against the culture.

What do you think are the events or ideas that can turn society round? Are these changes like a pendulum, which will in time swing back towards spirituality and morality and a sense of community?

Not everything is on a pendulum. I think some developments are linear. Technology and its impact on jobs, communications – some things have changed and will not go back.

In terms of morality, as individuals when we find we have gone too far we pull back. It's possible society may do that. I hope that crime reaches a pitch where society recoils. Examples in past societies indicate that might be possible. The worry is that people's tolerances are very different and some people may not reach that point.

I cannot believe it is a comfortable society that sits down and watches another depressing TV series and feels happy or warm at the end of it. It may be a reflection of life, but in some ways it's a sad reflection. People watch something truly horrific on television – yet another crime series in which people are ripped apart every night. We know it happens, though it doesn't happen as regularly as it does on television. Sooner or later, somebody says, "I've had enough of this."

Alistair Burt

How can we turn our society around and bring it back to more sensible values?

You don't bring it back: you move it on. Society is always moving on. I'm not one of those Conservatives who look back to a golden age. The golden age wasn't quite what people thought it was. You can't go back in any circumstances.

I think there is an open door in society at the moment. People are searching for all sorts of things. Just as we know that even the most unruly children appreciate limits to what they can do, I believe society is much the same. We've been through a period where the barriers have been dropped, and some of the restrictions of the past, the hypocrisies and the deferential attitudes that had to be challenged in a meritocratic, democratic society, were right to go.

The danger, of course, is that we've not put anything in their place. This, I think, is where the Church has a clear role to play – and other opinion-formers as well: I don't believe it's a role for any single group. We should be backing each other up. I would have thought that what people are searching for are these barriers, these signposts. The Church has got them all at its fingertips; it just needs to expound them. After all, it has the best manifesto.

Biography

Alistair Burt was born in 1955. He was educated at Bury Grammar School and at St John's College, Oxford, where he read law and was President of the Oxford University Law Society. He then practised as a solicitor.

In 1982 he was elected to Haringey Borough Council and a year later, in June 1983, was elected Member of Parliament for Bury North.

He was the secretary of the Conservative Back-bench Energy Committee from 1983 to 1985; national vice-chairman of the Tory Reform Group from 1985 to 1988; vice-chairman of the Conservative Back-bench European Affairs Committee from 1991 to 1992.

Between 1985 and 1990 he was Parliamentary Private Secretary to Kenneth Baker, in various departments.

He was Parliamentary Under-Secretary of State for Social Security from 1992 to 1995 and was appointed Sponsor Minister for Manchester and Salford in August 1994. In July 1995 he was appointed Minister of State at the Department of Social Security.

He is married and has a daughter and a son. His interests include football and modern art. He is secretary of the Parliamentary Christian Fellowship.

Two interviews were conducted on 1 March 1994 and 14 December 1995.

Simon Hughes

Did you have a Christian upbringing? What kind of childhood did you have?

My parents were simple Christians; they didn't make any great song and dance about their faith. Neither had been to university. My dad worked as a brewer. He got up at four o'clock in the morning and did shifts. My mum was in the Samaritans and the Red Cross. We were very much a community-minded family who did their bit.

My father's family had been gardeners and came from North Wales, which is our spiritual home – from beautiful places like Porthmadog and Maentwrog. Dad's buried there, as are all my paternal relatives. Emotionally, I feel very Welsh, even though we are other things as well.

The anomaly is that I was born and brought up in a village, and went to school in the mountains, and then ended up as one of the most urban MPs. Maybe all that village stuff contributes to my strong sense of the need for community where I am.

Somebody had said to me that I ought to be a lawyer because I was talkative and argued a lot. That seemed to be as good an idea as any other, and so I went through school thinking that was what I would do. It was only in my bar finals year that I was prompted to say, "My

93

commitment to Christ has got to come first," and I have held to that, however weak or however strong the flame has been, ever since.

It was a new sort of allegiance, like a love affair, I suppose. Suddenly your emotions change. Again, like a love affair, you don't retain the same level of excitement for the rest of your life, but you remember it, and it is the root of other things.

If you were studying for the law, why did you go into Parliament?

In a way I am there accidentally. I never expected to win, I hadn't really planned to stand. It hadn't been a career plan. I was doing far better as a barrister and would certainly have done far better, financially, than I have done since. But having got there, I thought, I have got to do the job.

I'd settled in Bermondsey. I had to live near my chambers because I didn't have any money and I had to cycle in. There I became involved in the community, campaigning to prevent the demolition of loads of houses, involved in the youth club with difficult teenagers.

The constituency is much more important to me than national politics. I took on its huge inequalities, huge deprivation, huge need, and in a way I became a lot of people's last resort, the embodiment of their hope. That gets to be a bit of a burden, but I felt for a long time that I had to honour what I had taken on. I have a highly developed sense of service – an over-developed sense, my friends tell me. To a degree, it comes from the family streak of Welsh Presbyterianism and puritanism.

94

It's all about not being self-indulgent and trying to look after others.

My colleagues are now within sight of taking control of the council, which is one bit of my unfinished business. If I could at least bring into being a different type of administration in Southwark, more pluralist and more community-based, I could walk away feeling I had achieved something visible locally. Huge boroughs don't relate to people at all.

But why did you become a Liberal?

There was a general election in 1966 and I knew I wasn't a Tory by then. Harold Wilson was in power. I remember it as an entirely unprincipled Government. I sent away for the manifestos and I read the Liberal manifesto and thought, This is extraordinary, I agree with all of this! I am obviously one of these.

Nationally, I feel Toryism has been tried and has failed. For me, the gospel is all about social reform, correcting the injustice that market forces always produce, and you can do that in various ways. I've always been unhappy with the way which was taught by economic socialism, which doesn't work and is also very overbearing. I believe in the richness of diversity in society, and, for me, socialism often kills that.

The alternative to a selfish, "hold on to what you've got" society is a redistributive society but one which doesn't prescribe that you have to do it "my way". Labour Party people say to me, "Come on, Simon, join us," and every time they imply that there is only one allegiance you can have if you have social and political objectives about equality and social justice. To me, that demonstrates exactly why liberal democracy as a political philosophy is needed. You need to recognise there are different ways to achieve a socially just government.

I see liberal democracy burgeoning around the world – in South America, Africa increasingly (with more difficulty), Asia. In my book, the battle is about how you regulate market forces and how much you give to the individual as opposed to the collective. For me, the Christian faith is about the accountability of the individual to others. The best available option is a welfare economy which accepts private enterprise but regulates it in the context of a recognition of the rights and freedoms of others. You have to add in the anger and determination of the gospel to deliver a much more radical agenda than some of my colleagues would prescribe. Some of them stop much earlier down the road of intervention and regulation than I would.

But is such a mix of free-ish markets and welfare capitalism sustainable in the face of globalisation?

Not in the same way, and not without being really brave about what we think and say.

I foresee that in my lifetime we may yet have no guaranteed state pension. I'm willing to argue that now because if you look where poverty is to be found, it is increasingly among the unemployed and single parents and decreasingly among pensioners. I think we have to assume that there are no unalterables at all in the provisions of the welfare state. There is no justification for the state paying a pension in a society where, more and more often, one comes with the job. That's why I prefer a safety net to guarantee a minimum income.

I'm not convinced that we can have a high-value, high-wage economy. The reality is that if we believe in global free trade – and it's difficult to stop it – we have to compete with the growing economies, particularly of the Pacific Rim, and that means we have to reduce our living standards in the long term.

And that is where the whole environmental debate comes in for me because it is about global equity. If I have a global or a national mission, as opposed to a local one (but they all tie in), it is to get on to every Government's agenda that the most important task is to reduce the gap between the haves and the have-nots. Unless we see that as a precondition of economic and social cohesion, there will be increasing injustice leading to civil disobedience and increasing alienation of the poor, whether in the middle of New York or the backwoods of Indonesia.

It is just ridiculous that many of the poorest countries of the world are still repaying more in debt than we give them. We have to have a much more just system. Kenneth Clarke and the Prime Minister, to be fair, have probably done as much as any of their predecessors on this. That's why international organisations are important, so that you can send people in to do peace-keeping: economic peace-keeping, which is about a soundly based IMF and World Bank; environmental peace-keeping, so you can go in and stop destruction in the name of the international community; ideally, a move towards civil and political peace-keeping, so you can go in and uphold human rights.

That's where the European Community has been so successful in many ways. We have a separate convention for the Continent that deals with human rights and can override domestic prejudice, and a set of legislation which means that when our environmental standards haven't been high enough, we've been pushed.

You have to accept the breakdown of sovereignty and the old order. If the UN was to fail, it would be a huge disaster. The major criticism you can make of it is that they have to get everybody on board. That's why the debates in Britain about majority voting and vetoes and sovereignty are so real. I am glad we are now into the debate about devolution and the United Kingdom's constitution. You have to accept that there will be some balances and some times when you are out-voted. It does mean the decline of the nation-state and a recognition of more natural communities.

The good thing about the history of the post-war world, I suppose, is the development of regional formations: the EU, the Organisation of African States, the North American Free Trade Association, the Organisation of American States and now the South Pacific countries. So there are good signs.

Everyone is saying we need to recover a sense of community. How is it going to happen?

You have to start at the bottom and work up. You can't prescribe things. I have a fairly simplistic view, which I have tested and it seems to work, that most people know the geographical community they belong to. But people may also have other communities which need to be recognised: faith communities, interest communities, work communities. Those should be the building blocks.

The wise politician should seek to establish what these communities are and work with them. If you start there, the rest will follow. If we take ten of my constituents at random, of different ages and backgrounds and faiths, I think you would find they agreed on their hierarchy of geographical community. They would say, "We belong in Vauxhall," or wherever. Then they would say, "We're Londoners." Then they would say, however recent arrivals they were, "We're British" – or they might say, "We're English," and that's an interesting question. And then, if you pushed them further, most of them would also accept they had a European and a global citizenship.

So I think most of the community allegiances are actually there, but politicians spend all their time distorting them, or fiddling around with them, or seeking to gerrymander them, often for political ends, rather than just listening and reflecting them.

Why do you think our communities have broken up?

They've broken up through some unavoidable and some avoidable causes. The unavoidable causes are things like mass communication, greater affluence, travel, education, people's willingness to go further for work – all perfectly proper things that make people less narrow in their view of where they belong. The avoidable things have been things that have forced people to go unnecessarily. In Southwark the housing-allocations policy keeps breaking down communities. It doesn't matter to the authority which bit of the borough you live in.

Other things haven't helped. The buildings of the

Sixties, where there is no shared space and you haven't a clue who else lives in your block. The tax system hasn't recognised enough the benefit of caring parents and families. We have encouraged some people to go to work when perhaps they ought to have been at home. And the Thatcher years encouraged people too much to be selfish and to go for their own satisfaction, without thinking of others.

And communities have to respect people's fears and histories. That failure has caused a lot of the avoidable problems of the last twenty or thirty years. A lot of people in my part of the world say, "We used to be our own people round here. Now we've got loads of blacks." They don't have antipathy towards any particular black family or person; what they are worried about is the fact that they suddenly have a community that isn't one they know or understand. You have to hear what people say who are "little Englanders" because unless we start from where they are, the argument that we are all an international community now will only force them to be defensive. They won't be if you take them with you.

All the biblical stuff about welcoming the refugees is fine, but you have to understand that if people at the bottom of the heap pay a greater price in terms of housing and jobs, it is not surprising they say, "Hang on a minute, we were the refugees in the last generation and we are the first people who have to suffer now."

Some people might accuse you of political incorrectness.

One of the battles I am determined to go on fighting is to return to a dialogue where you speak your prejudice

Simon Hughes

and start from there. Political correctness has been the bane of people working in multi-ethnic communities like mine. Positive discrimination has really made people aggressive and understandably so. If suddenly tomorrow the Government announced that every German living in Britain would be given £10 a week on their social security, the person announcing it would be lynched.

The Christian message is all about the value of belonging. Everyone is my brother or sister, but it doesn't mean there aren't people to whom you have a particular duty. Our society has inherited the Old Testament tradition of honouring your father and mother and your family – the people who are around you – and we have failed to do that.

Do you think that as a Christian you bring something unique to politics that can't be replicated by any other system of belief or ideology?

Yes. Christianity leads people to confront the truism of politics, that at the end of the day you have to account for your own decisions. The faith teaches that if you accept your own inadequacy, that is understood and taken into account. If the state reflected the gospel, it would say, "We know you are going to fail all the time, but our job is to go on building you up again."

And the state must never generalise. That is why I haven't been a socialist, because socialism traditionally puts too many people in the same basket. My political vision, inspired by Christian faith, says that everybody is different. The job of the politician should be to release the uniqueness of each individual – which is what the faith

101

is all about. It says, "Come to me as you are, uniquely different, created individual, and I will set you free. I will give you eternal life, the best option that is available."

My experience is that those beliefs that are held in common among Jews and Muslims and Christians actually mean that there is enormous solidarity there if anyone looks for it. I find that the people who probably understand best where I am coming from are Muslim friends as much as Christian friends. Just as the Church has been ruined by denominationalism, so faith and moral values and ethics have been ruined by divisions where often there is a commonality of belief.

One of the things I have learnt is that being a Christian, or describing yourself as one, doesn't guarantee the validity of the next sentence that comes from your mouth. I get letters all the time from Christians who say, for example, "I'm astounded that you say you are a Christian and yet you voted for abortion at twenty-four weeks." I have to write back and say, "Just show me in the gospel where it says that, given that abortions are going to happen – because you can never stop them – it should not be at twenty-four weeks."

John Smith, I think, said once that the job of politics is to convert ideas into practice and the job of the honest Christian politician is to interpret the gospel into a framework which permits people to make choices and protects them when they do so but doesn't make the choices for them.

We can't prescribe a Christian Utopia. We have to legislate for a fallen world. Yes, we are influenced by our faith and our beliefs, but I am the MP for 80,000 people, many of whom are non-Christians, many of whom have no faith and many of whom are people in circumstances entirely different from mine. They need a framework which is socially coherent for them, which enables and validates and develops them as individuals to be themselves – and, I hope, then gives them the opportunity to open the door marked "Salvation on offer through faith".

Some politicians have criticised the Church for meddling in politics at the expense of its real job. Do you think it is on the wrong track?

First, the Church has a duty to practise what Christ preached, and study of the Word and prayer and worship are crucial to that. So, the Church has that as its core function, which nobody else can do for it. Second, it is charged with working out the social gospel. I don't think the Church has spoken out clearly enough about that.

One of its greatest failures is denominationalism and sectarianism. The Church is a coalition, like any political party. The parallel is very clear. A political party divided does not win support; nor does a divided Church, which looks as if it has a Roman Catholic wing, an Anglican wing and an evangelical wing.

Its other weakness is that it has often failed to speak in the language of the day and to understand the next generation. There is some very good youth work, but by and large the Church has not moved as quickly as the rest of society. The message is the same – the miracle of the gospel is that Christ's teaching is entirely applicable now – but the Church just doesn't often communicate it in the language and style of today. It is like Parliament. Parliament is discredited because it clearly does not look or feel or sound like Britain.

103

What are the moral issues that concern you most, on which the Church should be speaking out?

The two fundamental things are inequality of wealth – because that is the test most people use of how just a society is – and the basic meeting of need, which for most people is housing. The health service, the education system and the transport system in general terms are good. The thing that is appallingly bad for a minority is a provision of secure housing. I can't understand how, fifty years after the war, we are still struggling to provide adequate housing for our country. It is disgraceful.

Globally, the Church again fails to address international inequity. How can we possibly leave the Brandt Commission agenda for so long and do nothing about it? Look at the protests about the Criminal Justice Bill and veal crates and so on. We are in an age now when people are not politically aligned; they don't trust parties very much, but they are willing to pick up the issue they think is important. If the Church wants to be where it is at, it has to be in there on those issues, leading and supporting. And it can do it, very well.

Isn't the problem that the Church sees freedom as freedom in God to do good whereas liberal democracy sees freedom as freedom of choice? How are you going to mobilise people in a democracy to choose to do good?

People are free to choose, bounded by the limits that the Government sets down. Society is always going to put some restrictions on people's freedom and, I hope, enforce them. You have to win the hearts and minds of people to a set of policies that actually inhibit the exploitation and abuses arising from choice. That's the much more difficult part. But you can't do it any other way. You can't say, "You will not smoke. You will not work more than twelve hours a week," or whatever. That just doesn't work in an educated society. People can see their way round it. You can't enforce such laws.

You have to accept the natural instinct to work and earn money. In Britain the unofficial economy is huge because you can't regulate those things. So you have to learn. That is where the politicians have failed. They have failed to produce a collective vision of where we could do better. It is one of the paradoxes of the democrat that the best way to deliver that (although you have to be terribly careful) is by personal leadership and example. The dilemma is that if people put their trust in an individual, which in a mass-communication age they will do increasingly, then there are all the dangers of the vulnerability of the individual. The higher the baboon goes up the tree, the more we see of his arse. I think the societies that work have a strong political leader who can unify the country around an agenda.

Why has there been a failure of moral leadership in our country – in all areas, not just in politics?

I think the reason is that within recent times people have chosen the wrong issues. Mrs Thatcher chose an issue that in the end was fundamentally wrong because it was selfish. When John Major tried "Back to Basics", he tried an issue that was sort of rightly conceived but wrongly thought through: what he actually meant was the core values that hold society together, but it got interpreted as the core moral principles by which we should live.

Some of our best politicians are people who have known public failings: people knew that Lloyd George had a mistress, and they knew that Winston Churchill drank all the time. But neither of them tried to say, "I'm morally better than you." Instead they united people round a social agenda. You have to pick a social agenda, not a personal agenda.

The Church, then, has to try to work on people's personal agendas and meet them where they are and deal with them separately. If only it could get that separation right, it could say, "Look, we are concerned about two things: the collective well-being, that God's world should have as much evidence of justice as possible, and the individual's personal attainment." In many countries it still does set the social agenda but it doesn't say, "This is conditional on you coming and joining us."

And yet some Christians will say, "How can you reform a secular society and revive its sense of community and altruism unless you first restore a belief in God?" What other motivation can you call on that is more powerful than self-interest?

The reason why I am a Christian is that, in my view, if you look around for principles that will give you the answers to all these things, you don't find anything coherent other than in that faith. There are two things that most people find the most difficult in their lives: their relationships with other people and their relationship with their Creator.

Now, people who don't have that dimension of the relationship between Creator and created can look around for a personal moral and ethical code, and they may arrive at a similar place, and many do, but there are no firmnesses there. So the Church is right to say that there is no conclusive, coherent agenda other than ours. It has been tested, and, properly understood, sensitively applied, intelligently explained, it works. And it doesn't even require you to sign up. Many people who can understand and accept the source of its agenda may take much longer to reach personal faith. But, without that, we are not going to resolve the questions. For me, all the politics in the world and all the manifestos in the world only ever get you so far because they are inadequate. They don't deal with a bit of you.

My political philosophy is about enabling people to develop their full talent. My Christian faith says that the crucial part of developing your full talent is that you actually take for yourself a faith as well. Without that, you can be very well rounded but you will not be fundamentally fulfilled. The same applies to society. That's why the Church has to work very hard to get people to sign up to that particular agenda, and why it has to be very bold about how it does it.

In the meantime politicians, Christian and non-Christian, have to seek to implement the social gospel, which there is much wider agreement about and which, in my view, is really the only alternative to the antisocial political message, which is self-centred. You just need courageous leadership to do that.

Belief in Politics

Biography

Simon Hughes was born in 1951. He was educated at Llandaff Cathedral School, Cardiff, Christ College, Brecon, and Selwyn College, Cambridge. He then attended the Inns of Court School of Law, taking his Bar finals in 1974, and the College of Europe in Bruges, where he took a Certificate in Higher European Studies in 1975.

He was a trainee at the EEC in Brussels 1975–6, a trainee and member of the Secretariat at the Directorate and Commission on Human Rights, Council of Europe, Strasbourg, 1976–7. Called to the Bar in 1974, he practised as a barrister from 1978.

He was elected Member for Bermondsey at the by-election of February 1983 and is currently MP for Southwark and Bermondsey. In the 1992 election his was the largest Liberal Democrat majority in England.

He was party spokesperson on the environment, 1983–8; health, January-June 1987; education, science and training, 1988–90; environment, natural resources and food, 1990–94. He is currently party spokesperson on the Church of England and on community and urban affairs and young people. He has also been Liberal Democrat Deputy Whip since 1989.

He has several joint publications to his name, including *Human Rights in Western Europe: The Next Thirty Years* (1981), *Across the Divide: Liberal Values for Defence and Disarmament* (1986) and *Pathways to Power* (1992).

This interview was conducted on 17 January 1995.

Peter Lilley

How have your Christian convictions shaped you?

I was brought up in a Christian family. Then I had the advantage of studying science at school and university, and whereas some of my fellow pupils were levered off any religious conviction they had by the argument that science had discredited it all, scientists can see that's nonsense. It's almost a premise of the scientific approach that you are in an orderly universe, and it's natural to see that as well as a physical order there is a spiritual and moral order – though ultimately it's a matter of faith rather than logical deduction.

Like a pair of spectacles, Christianity enables you to see things more clearly. It doesn't make you a better person, but you see the moral and spiritual dimensions of life and then have the challenge of living up to them. Most of us fall pretty short, but it's hard to wish to discard them, any more than, since I recently acquired glasses, I wish to go back to seeing things fuzzily.

Belief in Politics

The Church has sometimes seemed to be the unofficial opposition. Have you found that an irritation?

No, I think it's partly that the media will pick up critical comments and highlight them. I don't complain about that; it's part of the media's job. And though some of my colleagues sometimes tell the bishops to stop pontificating on political matters, I don't see that you can say there is an area of politics which has no religious dimension but everything else does. Clearly, everything has a religious dimension.

I think Christians of a conservative disposition should also make their views and values and interpretation of events known, and do so from an overtly Christian perspective. I don't think Christianity leads inevitably to being a Tory any more than to being a socialist, but you can be a Tory and see these things from a Christian perspective and illuminate public debate from that perspective. There is some clear overlap: a belief that Man is a fallen animal, that we don't expect perfectibility in this world and that therefore we have to try to organise society in a way that accommodates Man's selfishness as well as his higher instincts and aptitudes.

Perhaps that comes particularly naturally to the conservative end of the political spectrum. The left would tend, I think, to look towards the creation of the Kingdom of God on earth, and I don't think that is possible by political means – though I respect the Christian motivation of those who are perhaps over-ambitious in those directions.

Peter Lilley

But is it not also over-ambitious to put your faith in freedom of choice when people are fallen and are going to choose things that are demonstrably not good for them?

Well, the great thing about the market – and why it is congenial to Conservatives and, I think, conservative Christians – is that it allows for selfishness. It doesn't require it, and it's a mistake of the critics of the free-market position to suppose that the more selfish people are, the better it works: that's not it. It allows for selfishness in that you can prosper in a competitive free market only by satisfying the wants and needs of others and doing so more efficiently with less use of the nation's resources than others. So it harnesses even selfishness for the common good, as well as, in a free society, leaving opportunity for altruism and creative urges – which are very much part of the economic process.

It's absurd to suppose that every entrepreneur is purely money-grubbing and selfish. Some are, but many are actually rather creative individuals and want to satisfy the needs of others.

There may be other aspects of choice – you cannot have total freedom. Even the market requires an underlying morality. Essentially it works only when there is good faith and a respect for the rights of others: if everybody is bent on fraud and deceit, the system will not work effectively.

By contrast, sometimes virtue is its own reward. The Quakers were commercially successful because it was known that they – rather uniquely in their age – put an immensely high store by keeping their word in spirit as well as letter. People wanted to do business with people they could trust, and the trust, and the habit of trust, spread. That's an example of good moral behaviour driving out bad within a free society.

Christians who believe in the free market praise the biblical virtues of honesty and trust, but maybe do not appeal so much to justice – yet that is a strong theme in the Bible. Isn't that so?

I suppose the ultimate anarcho-capitalist would say nothing is justifiable if it's the result of coercion, and therefore any welfare provision that relies on the coercive power of the state to raise taxes and so on is not justifiable. Well, I'm not an anarcho-capitalist, so I don't have to argue my way out of that hole.

Clearly, I would like to rely on coercion as little as possible in general, but there is a clear obligation on those who are well-off and able to look after themselves to help those who are not able to look after themselves for any reason. I can't really envisage us not having the convenience of a welfare state to fulfil that obligation.

That fulfils, as it were, the minimum obligation of the Christian. He may feel he's got obligation over and above paying his taxes and meeting needs that way. There's no doubt that the assistance one person can give a neighbour directly counts more than a similar amount given through the rather anonymous structures of the state. But the two aren't alternatives in large measure.

Peter Lilley

You have quoted Samuel Johnson's maxim that the true test of a civilised society is generous provision for the poor. Is that a test we should apply to the current Government?

Yes, I think to any Government. That isn't to say that the more money you spend on welfare, the more virtuous you are (though on that scale we would clearly win because we are the highest-spending Government in terms of welfare there's ever been in this country).

What one has got to have is a system that provides a decent level to those in need, that is focused on those in need, that doesn't at the same time hand it out in a way that traps people in dependency or give to people who don't need it, who may thereby find their incentives to provide for themselves undermined, and so on. There is always a balancing act to be done.

The Church seems to see the poor as a higher priority than this Government does. Is that true?

I do talk with some Church groups, and I think one has to distinguish between the activists who are full-time on these problems, who are often a little detached from the normal attitudes of the congregation, which are more realistic – simultaneously generous, but they realise there are countervailing forces that have got to be taken into account in particular situations.

I do find a degree of unrealism in some Church circles who just suppose there is a bottomless purse, who are completely oblivious to the amount we spend. I might point out to them that the welfare state costs every working person £15 every working day. They think I must be telling a lie: it cannot be true because they all *know* that the Conservative Government is mean, and that is an unbelievably large sum of money. It's quite healthy to have dialogue in these matters just to get the facts established.

None the less, a lot of people, particularly in parish work, have more realistic views about the difference between people in need and the people who simply want to take money off other tax-payers. There, I think, it's perfectly possible to have a sensible dialogue.

Unfortunately, there is an element that identifies the needs of the poor with the interests of public-sector provision. They think that anything that expands public-sector provision must be in the interests of the poor.

That identity is not one-for-one. There is a need for public-sector provision, and it has to be at the right level and geared in the right way, but the best thing that can happen to the poor, of course, is self-reliance, if they are able to rise to it. If they're physically or mentally unable to, if there are no jobs, then we have to help them.

The best way for those who can help themselves is to enable them to help themselves, to encourage them and try to get the economy working. But the presumption of a lot of rather simplistic thinking is that poor people need things given to them rather than that the norm will be being helped for the period of unavoidable poverty. They will ultimately help themselves. Funnily enough, I find absolutely no difficulty talking to the Jewish community about that. They take that as the norm, and it would be terribly insulting to assume that the norm is that they would have more and more given to them.

Peter Lilley

Over the last twenty years families and neighbourhoods have changed beyond recognition. There is a statistic that 60 per cent of all households in Britain are now single-person households. Is that an exaggeration?

It is. It sounds as if it's because people are not married, but it's not that. I mean, my mother is a single-person household because my father died twenty years ago, but that is perfectly traditional. It's just that people leave home earlier and live longer now. There is a problem, but it's not measured by that statistic. The fact is, there are roughly 1.3 million single parents in this country against 20 million households. That is a huge increase but it's still not 60 per cent.

There is a direct problem that I, given my responsibilities for social security, have to address. A million of those 1.3 million are dependent on income support, and of the remaining 300,000 a high proportion are dependent on other benefits. So they are predominantly dependent on the tax-payer, and very few are receiving any support from the absent parent – usually the father. Hence the establishment of the Child Support Agency to ensure that both parents make a proper contribution towards the upkeep of their children, which is not proving as popular as some people imagined. It is no great surprise to me that there would be resentment and resistance from people to paying the full cost of supporting the children they have chosen to bring into this world.

There have been some problems, but one has to recognise that a lot of the articles are written by journalists who themselves – or whose friends – are recipients of demands. It's very significant that all the anti-articles are written by men and all the pro-articles by women – and, of course,

115

we hear very little at all from the children, who are the people who have to be our ultimate concern.

What do you think has caused the breakdown of the family in the last two decades?

It must be an interaction of economic, social, moral and spiritual attitudes. There have been major economic and social changes – forces which even in the absence of any change in attitude would have had an impact, I think. But also, sadly, many people take a view of life which is less other-directed, less prepared to say, "My first commitment is my child and my second commitment is myself."

And, because of that, a number of families split up, as it were for the convenience of the parents who, in other circumstances and given other values, would put the future of their child first and would see the joint commitment to bringing up that child together as itself a higher good than the psychic satisfaction they get from each other's company.

I heard Frank Field say at a conference we were both addressing – he happens to be a Labour politician but shares the same Christian perspective as I do – that the Christian basis of the family is that it's the body in which one learns about, and is based on, love. The state can't provide love and can't provide that foundation and teaching and experience. The state can only provide justice (perhaps I wouldn't use the word "justice"), can only provide some sort of economic rights.

We have to step in where families split up and try to ensure that the child has the proper resources to support him or her. But that's, as it were, a second-best: that's all the state can provide, the second-best. The Church (in the widest sense of the word) can convey belief in love and see the family as a channel for it, and it should be boosting that message.

Sadly, too often the Church just forgets about that and tries to second-guess us on the business of economic rights and justice, which it's perfectly entitled to do as well, but not instead of the primary message, which the Church can put over ten times more effectively than any politician.

But might not the Conservative emphasis on self-interest contribute to the breakdown of community if it spills over from economic thinking into social affairs?

Yes. I am not a believer in atomistic individualism: that everybody should simply pursue their own self-interest (or we could even bear it if they did) without any altruistic feelings, any willingness to subordinate their own immediate interest to that of others, and particularly their family.

To the extent that those attitudes that denigrate commitment to others undermine that, that must be corrosive of society as a whole. I sometimes see people writing that Thatcherism preached selfishness and that that has led to people behaving more selfishly and has undermined the family. I honestly think that's bunkum. I don't think, by and large, people read some obscure remarks by Mrs Thatcher in a woman's magazine about the non-existence of society (when she was actually making the point about personal responsibility) and immediately changed their behaviour and left their wives and abandoned their children – it's just absurd.

If we had that much influence on society, then I'd give a few sermons and, *bang*, the whole of society would be reformed. People don't base their behaviour on what a few politicians say. They are more likely to base it, even in these days, on the moral tone which a bishop or a priest or a devout lay person can convey.

Isn't the point that the whole tenor of society has been altered so that individual self-interest is seen as the main driving force?

No, I don't think so – and, in fact, if you're going to be materially successful in the marketplace, you are going to have to convince your customers that their interest is pre-eminent. If you convince them that you're actually putting your own interest first, they are probably not going to remain customers for long. So that whole ethos of the market does require the ethos of service.

Secondly, the pursuit of self-interest collectively, through syndicates, trades unions and public-sector bodies, is just as selfish as the pursuit of it individualistically. In a world where everybody is organised into collective groups, that leads to the destruction of society as people pursue their collective self-interest aggressively and aren't prepared to enter into any give-and-take with others.

The presumption that organising things collectively is morally superior I just think is wrong in theory and self-evidently refuted in practice. We saw it in the "winter of discontent": people not burying the dead and so on.

That was the pursuit of collective self-interest: just as bad as the pursuit of personal self-interest.

Why has our society become so cynical about its leaders? Do you think there has been a failure of leadership?

There does seem, for reasons I don't fully understand, to be an unleashing of cynicism. I think scepticism about politicians is highly desirable. Countries where too much is expected of, and too much faith is put in, political leaders are not the sorts of societies I would like to live in. They tend to be authoritarian, fascistic or totalitarian.

If you look back, there's always been a great deal of scepticism about politicians in this country, and that's a good thing and should continue. But it does seem to have moved, over a fairly short period, to the straight cynical, negative, nihilistic approach. It may burn itself out in a matter of months or years, I don't know.

I don't quite know why it should be. The only reason I can think of, because it seems to be a worldwide rather than a purely British phenomenon, is that simultaneously you've had a very long, bruising recession which has made people pretty fed-up – I can well understand that – coupled with the collapse of the whole Cold War confrontation, the sense of an external enemy which required a degree of internal solidarity. Maybe that has meant that people, particularly in the media and the "chattering classes", now feel free to be wholly destructive. That's not an argument I have tested rigorously, so it may turn out to be without any great value.

Belief in Politics

Do you still believe that the Conservative Party can offer this country a moral vision?

I don't think a political party should be the source of a moral vision, but, equally, a party which tried to offer a policy or approach which was devoid of moral content would be selling the electorate short. It's impossible, in any case, to have a political view which doesn't have a moral content. You have to take views about things like responsibility: we have to make moral choices.

The sad thing about political debate recently, which has always been a weakness of moral debate in this country, is the equation between morality and sexual morality. Sexual morality is part of morality, of course, but there are seven deadly sins, as I recall. In an interview, as soon as I mention the moral dimension of conservatism, the interviewer says: "Oh, you're talking about morality, are you, Mr Lilley? Sex!" It's degenerate, really.

What is particularly sad now is seeing newspapers which pose as having a high moral tone, like the *Independent*, using the excuse of a slogan to move their gossip column on to the front page. In a free market people can choose to make their living by pandering to the lowest possible tastes, but they don't have to. They can choose some other way.

I think what the press has been doing recently is fairly squalid, but you just have to put up with it. My view is that the harm done by trying to introduce forms of censorship would be far greater than the gains to be got by it. It would backfire. It would be seen as politicians changing the law to protect their own reputations. If we could pass a law saying they were not allowed to write about the private lives of people in general, everybody would know what they really meant was the private lives of politicians. They don't write about Mrs Bloggs of 13 Acacia Avenue; they write about people who are in the public eye.

If democracy needs a free and unmuzzled press, the only protection a public figure has got is moral rectitude. Do you believe, then, that public figures should behave more morally than private citizens?

No, I wouldn't expect a higher or lower standard of politicians than of anybody else. Obviously, everybody ought to strive for the highest possible standards in their personal life, but we know we are all fallen creatures and we will all fall short. When we go to church one of the first things we do is confess our sins, and that presupposes we have committed some. It's amazing to me that editors of newspapers are surprised when they find that sin is quite a prevalent thing.

They're only interested in one kind of sin for some reason – why that should be, I don't know. There are lots of other sins they might turn their attention to in due course, and they'll undoubtedly find we're all guilty of something.

Anger is one of the seven deadly sins – it seems to me a bad one. Are they going to suddenly turn their attention to that and we'll all have to resign if we've ever lost our tempers? You could say, "I don't want to be led by politicians who are prone to anger." It's probably more of a read-across than whether they are prone to falling into bed with their twenty-two-year-old research assistants.

Belief in Politics

How would you sum up your own Christian vision of public life?

Your Christian values will influence you in two ways. One will be in your choice of objectives and the other in your choice of means.

In some ways, there's a clearer influence on your choice of means, by which I mean the way in which you conduct yourself politically. It ought to be more incumbent upon you to try to be honest. I'm not saying that any of us is 100 per cent candid because the pressures make you slip into distortions and half-truths a lot of the time; but you should feel compelled to try and avoid doing so, and that's an important influence in the way you conduct business and also in the way you treat your opponents. I disagree with my opponents, but one should try not to fall into the trap of imputing the worst possible motive to them.

I suspect my objectives would be fairly similar to those of Tony Blair or Gordon Brown. We want to see a better society, with proper provision for those in need. I would perhaps put more emphasis on freedom of choice and personal responsibility than they would, but that would be a matter of degree. It's how all the policy ramifications of that then work out that lead us to rather different philosophical views.

One wing of the Christian debate would tend to see that you can bring about the Kingdom of God on earth by political means. I think that's wrong because political means are essentially coercive and if the movement towards the Kingdom of God comes in men's hearts, it's not going to come through coercion.

It has to be said that if people are changed in their

hearts, then that will undoubtedly change society, but it won't be brought about by political changes.

Biography

Peter Lilley was born in 1943 and educated at Dulwich College and Clare College, Cambridge, from which he graduated with a degree in natural sciences and economics.

Formerly a director with Greenwell Montagu, he was an economic adviser on underdeveloped countries from 1966 to 1972 and an investment adviser on North Sea oil and other energy industries from 1972 to 1984.

He was chairman of the Bow Group from 1972 to 1975 and consultant director of the Conservative Party's research department from 1979 to 1983.

In that year he was elected MP for St Albans and served as a member of the Parliamentary Select Committee on Treasury and Civil Service Matters and as secretary to the Conservative Back-bench Energy Committee.

In 1984 he became Parliamentary Private Secretary to Lord Bellwin and William Waldegrave, the Ministers for Local Government, and until 1987 worked as PPS to the then Chancellor of the Exchequer, Nigel Lawson.

In 1987 he became Economic Secretary at the Treasury and, in 1989, Financial Secretary. A year later he entered the Cabinet as Secretary of State for Trade and Industry and was appointed a Privy Councillor.

He was given his present portfolio of social security, the largest budget in the Government, in the spring of 1992.

He has several publications to his name, including *Do You Sincerely Want to Win?* (1972), *Lessons for Power*

Belief in Politics

(1974), *Delusions of Income Policy* (with Samuel Britten, 1977) and, for the Centre for Policy Studies, *Thatcherism: The Next Generation* (1989).

This interview was conducted on 1 March 1994.

John Major

What were the principal influences that shaped your view of the world and your moral vision?

My moral commitments are largely drawn from my parents, who instilled in me from an early age a love of our country, the difference between right and wrong and the responsibilities of the strong to care for the weak.

My early years in Brixton had a profound effect on me – in particular, the uncertainty and insecurity I experienced as a result of the failure of my parents' business and their ensuing ill-health. I hope that has given me an empathy for those who are forced, through no fault of their own, to endure physical, mental or financial hardship.

During my time as a councillor in Lambeth, I saw at first hand the abject failure of municipal socialism as it robbed individuals and families of dignity, self-respect and opportunity. Socialism sapped the enterprise, drive, initiative and hope of so many of our inner cities. And the struggle against the Soviet socialist system too, which was the backdrop to my upbringing, reinforced my belief in our system of democracy.

Belief in Politics

Do you believe in God?

Yes, I do believe. I don't pretend to understand all of the complex parts of Christian theology, but I simply accept it.

I have a simple belief that the individual comprises three distinct elements: body, mind and soul. To be without an appreciation of all three is to be without a full understanding of the fullness of life and the purpose of living.

Do you ever pray, and in what circumstances?

Yes, in all circumstances.

Politicians seem to be held in low esteem in our society, and yet we rely on their leadership. What are the qualities you most admire in a leader?

Honesty, wisdom, integrity, compassion, perseverance. Leadership is about setting a course you believe to be right and pursuing it even if it is unpopular and not to your political advantage.

But I don't accept your presupposition. As a constituency MP, I know how much the work of elected representatives is appreciated and valued by those who call on us for help. Sadly, much of the bipartisan, non-party-political work which goes on inside and outside Parliament or the Council Chamber is never reported.

If politicians were held in low esteem, I don't believe

that almost 80 per cent of those eligible to vote at a general election would do so. It's true that I did become concerned, following a few incidents involving MPs, that there was a growing unease about a perceived reduction of standards in public life, so I asked Lord Nolan to chair an inquiry into standards in public life, to reassure the public. A large proportion of his recommendations have already been implemented.

Is it possible to keep the private behaviour of a politician separate from his or her public responsibilities?

We all have our faults, but mistakes which involve a betrayal of trust are especially worrying. The important questions are, first, what does a particular mistake by a politician tell you about his or her character and, secondly, how will that mistake impact on his or her job? It clearly can't be right for a politician to say one thing and do another in his private life.

Are there any circumstances under which a politician would be right to lie?

Honesty and integrity are essential in retaining the bond of trust between Parliament and Government and between parliamentarians and their constituents. To be found guilty of knowingly misleading the House of Commons is still the most serious charge which can be levelled against any politician. There will be circumstances, particularly relating to national interest and national security, when it may not be possible to give the full picture or, indeed, to comment at all.

Belief in Politics

Do you think that poverty is inevitable in any society? What difference in income between the rich and the poor do you think is acceptable?

We shouldn't accept anyone living in poverty in the United Kingdom. We have one of the most comprehensive safety nets in the world, and benefits have increased in terms of their purchasing power since 1979 and are, perhaps, more rigorously targeted. Next year the social-security budget alone will be £97 billion, with a further £51 billion on health and social services. To put these figures in context, the total receipts from income tax amount to £70 billion.

A small number do slip through the net – they're people who live beyond the normal conventions of life, and we seek to bring them back within them.

I believe that in a healthy and just society our attention should be focused on the levels of care and assistance we provide for the poorest, rather than on differentials between rich and poor. Our political opponents say we ought to be spending more in these areas, yet they fail to say how they would raise it and by how much.

You yourself made your way in society without the privileges of a private education. What do you make of the fact that private education is still so closely linked with success in later life?

There is much less evidence of private education *per se* leading to success in later life in modern Britain. What advantage there is, I would suggest, is probably due to the emphasis on moral integrity, self-discipline and public service which is found in many of our best public schools – and I've made no secret of my wish to see all our schools embrace these values.

Freedom of choice for the individual has been one of the central moral commitments of Conservative Governments in recent years. Is freedom of choice always a good idea?

Giving individuals and families choice, I believe, raises standards among those providing the goods and services and also strengthens individuals by encouraging them to take greater responsibility.

But I don't accept that freedom of choice is *always* a good thing. The evidence for that is the way Parliament spends so much time legislating and regulating to prevent people from choosing to commit crime, for example.

To what extent has the rise of consumerism contributed to the fracturing of community values in the recent past?

I do believe there has been a fracturing of community values in Britain since the war, but I don't accept that blame can be laid exclusively at the door of consumerism. Living standards in this country have doubled since the Fifties, and people have used their greater disposable incomes to purchase new homes. The massive expansion in car ownership has meant that people no longer need to live close to their place of work, family and friends. The expansion of telecommunications has had a similar effect.

We mustn't underestimate, too, the impact of television both inside the home and outside.

But none of these material possessions should be viewed as having a wholly negative effect on community values. Taken together, they have changed the nature of communities throughout the world.

Economists in the United States have recently begun to find new ways to measure national wellbeing, on the basis that Gross National Product is not an adequate guide. What aspects of national life do you think are good indicators of our wellbeing?

I believe that the indicators of the moral and spiritual well-being of society already exist. On the positive side, there is the increased giving in time and money to charitable and civic causes, and concern for the environment. On the negative side, there is the alarming increase in family breakdown and the increase in crime and the fear of crime. The good news is that we have just had the largest fall in recorded crime since records began over a century ago.

To what do you attribute the fragmentation of the family in modern Britain?

There are several social factors which, without doubt, have contributed to the breakdown of the family, and one of them has been the greater social freedom and financial independence enjoyed in this country since the war. Much of this greater financial independence has come from the welfare state. This is the paradox that Lord Skidelsky has pointed out, that the welfare state has actually contributed to the break-up of the family.

Then there is the dispersion of the wider family, whereas fifty years ago grandparents, aunts and uncles would often live in close proximity to each other and could be on hand to assist with the considerable demands and pressures involved in raising a family.

Other factors would include society's increasing acceptance of divorce and separation, and the devaluing of the role of the mother.

Why did you start your "Back to Basics" campaign? What basic values are necessary for a healthy, free and just society?

When I first used the phrase "back to basics" in my speech at the Conservative Party conference in 1993, I was seeking to articulate a mood in society at large which had lost confidence in the permissive, politically correct, value-free society which had its roots in the Sixties. I sensed that people wished to return to basic core values and old certainties which had served previous generations well.

Nowhere was this feeling more clearly exposed than in our state education system, where the emphasis in recent years has been on a value-free education and experiential, child-centred learning. Parents wanted their children to go to school to be taught how to read and write, and to be taught the difference between right and wrong.

Belief in Politics

Our society is said to have no common moral vision. To what extent do you think this can be attributed to a decline in religious belief?

I am sure it is possible to draw some correlation between the decline in church attendance and a rise in social ills. However, that is not the same as saying that religious belief is in decline. I recall that a recent survey found that 85 per cent of those questioned believed in God. We should recognise, too, that many millions of people watch or listen to religious broadcasting on television or radio. There is evidence that religious belief is now on the increase, and I would anticipate that this will feed through into the moral fabric of the nation.

It is, of course, possible for individuals to draw upon the social values of Christianity without being Christians. We can all offer many examples of people apparently without faith who abide by Christian principles in their daily life and often put those with faith to shame. What I would say, though, is that faith adds life, reason and context to a set of rules.

Do you think church leaders have a right to criticise political decisions on moral grounds?

Yes. They have as much of a right to express their opinions as anyone else in a free and democratic society. But they should also address the spiritual poverty in modern-day society. I would like to see much greater partnership between the Church and the state at all levels to rebuild the moral and social fabric of our society as we prepare for the next millennium.

John Major

The "new" Labour Party seems to be increasingly influenced by Christianity. Does the Christian faith exert similar influence within the Conservative Party?

The Conservative Party is founded on principles flowing from the Christian faith. I very much agree with Baroness Blatch when she said recently to the Conservative Christian Fellowship, "I believe there is a wider agreement than is often supposed around a core set of values. For those of the Christian faith, that core can be found in the Ten Commandments, the Sermon on the Mount and Christ's call to love our neighbours as ourselves. They have become enriched by two thousand years of accumulated wisdom and doctrine, and in today's society you must look at how these are relevant to everyday life, and how they can be interpreted. I believe that a core of values for today should focus on a sense of self-reliance and self-discipline, an acceptance of responsibility for one's actions, a regard to proper authority, a sense of unselfishness, honesty, dignity, fairness and loyalty, and the readiness to stand up for what one believes in. These are a set of values which encapsulate Christian and Conservative thinking."

But no one political party can hope to claim exclusivity on Christian principles.

In what ways do you see Britain changing over the next ten years?

Prophecy and politics are rather different subjects, but I am sure the improvements which have been achieved over the last decade will continue, provided we don't abandon the principles on which they were based.

Belief in Politics

In the Seventies, Britain was regarded as the sick man of Europe. Strikes brought the country to a standstill. Inflation hit all-time highs. Nationalised industries were, by and large, inefficient and were run mainly for the benefit of the employees rather than the customers. All that is now behind us because of the tough decisions and determination of our Government. We have now seen the longest period of low inflation for fifty years, the lowest basic rate of tax for over fifty years, the lowest mortgage rates for thirty years and more of our people in jobs and fewer unemployed than in any other major European economy. Days lost to strikes have fallen to their lowest level since records began. Exports are at record levels and Britain is number one in Europe for foreign investment.

Much more remains to be done, but the position we have reached offers great opportunity for the future. The key to that future is enterprise at the heart of a free and prosperous society. During the next ten years, I look forward to this enterprise culture increasing. The core of enterprise is not government but individuals – individuals inspired by a dream of what might be. Remember, it wasn't government that invented the steam engine, the telephone, the motor car, the radio. It wasn't government that built British railways.

But the spirit of enterprise isn't confined to inventors who change the world. It's what makes thousands of people set up small businesses every year, putting their security and lives on the line because they think they have an idea that will work. If we want to be a successful society, we must succeed in freeing, exciting, stimulating individuals to the limits of their achievement. That means putting aside the old culture of disparaging success and

134

those who aspire to it. If we want to be a successful society, we can't afford to be an envious society.

We mustn't interpret enterprise narrowly. It's not just a business culture; it's a set of values that can be expressed in countless other ways too. It can be expressed in charities, sports clubs, schools, hospitals and throughout the public service. It's a myth that enterprise creates a selfish and greedy society. It's a myth that society can only be made fair and just by bureaucracy, meddling and corporatism. It's a myth that you can make the weak stronger by making the strong weaker.

Above all, we must ensure that our enterprise culture is accompanied and driven by those basic, core values which served us so well in the past – values which ensure a much more caring attitude, looking after the less fortunate in society.

Biography

John Major was born in 1943 and educated at Rutlish Grammar School.

From 1960, when he joined the Conservative Party, to 1969, he held various offices at the Brixton Conservative Association; he was its chairman from 1970 to 1971.

Between 1965 and 1981 he was an executive of the Standard Chartered Bank.

He became a councillor for the London Borough of Lambeth in 1968.

In both elections of 1974 he contested St Pancras North for the Conservative Party. In 1979 he was elected as Member of Parliament for Huntingdonshire and since 1983 has been the Member for Huntingdon.

Belief in Politics

From 1981 to 1983 he was the Parliamentary Private Secretary to Timothy Raison and Patrick Mayhew, Ministers of State at the Home Office. From 1983 to 1985 he was Government Whip. His other Government posts included Minister of State for Social Security and the Disabled and Chief Secretary of the Treasury.

From 1989 to 1990 he was Chancellor of the Exchequer. In November 1990 he was elected leader of the Conservative and Unionist Party. He has been Prime Minister since 1990.

His interests include rugby, cricket, football, and opera. He is married and has one son and one daughter.

This was a written interview rather than a face-to-face interview. We received the complete manuscript in response to our written questions on 31 January 1996.

John Redwood

You are often described as a right-wing politician. Is that accurate?

I don't think the labels "right-wing" and "left-wing" are particularly meaningful in many areas. I am a traditional Conservative, and Conservatism for me blends several different strands of thought. I believe in limited government; I believe that currently government is too big. But I also believe in government doing those things which only government can do. You need a strong criminal law code, for example. I mix belief in the importance of defending the nation and the citizen against disorder, which requires strong state power, with saying we need far less state power in areas like industrial and economic management, where markets are much better at deciding the future.

I also believe in our institutional heritage; you only change an institution if it is self-evidently in need of reform. Otherwise you should leave it untouched and pass it on to future generations.

Belief in Politics

What are the philosophical or political influences that shaped your thinking?

I think the biggest influence on me was a negative one. I was brought up under the evil spectre of communism, and the struggles of my student generation were about communist aggression in the world and how the West should respond to that. The first political event I really remember, indelibly imprinted on my mind, was the Cuban missile crisis, when the world held its breath; I certainly held mine. We were all amazed and relieved when Kennedy stood his ground and emerged as a figure of immense strength who showed that the West could defend freedom.

That got me reading the philosophy that lay behind Marxism. I found it fairly incredible that people could believe it. It seemed so flawed, in terms of both its history and its economics, so I set about trying to help bring it down.

I knew we'd really won when a friend of mine was invited to become the privatisation adviser to Fidel Castro. If you'd said to me, even ten years ago when I was embarking on taking the message about free enterprise round the world, that a friend of mine would soon be invited in by Castro to advise on privatisation, I'd have thought you were mad. That is the extent of the victory over this evil.

In the Sixties there were a lot of liberals and lefties in Britain who were fellow-travellers of communism and who would say, "Of course, we don't really agree with the suppression of parliaments, but it's probably a price worth paying because it will mean that these countries are much more successful economically. They're clearly

138

going to outpace us." It was only twenty years later that the whole dream was in ruins and we saw that the East had fallen cruelly behind, economically as well as spiritually and in terms of lost freedoms. An experiment on a heroic scale had destroyed the lives of a couple of generations of people.

Harold Wilson's "great white heat of the technological revolution" speech was about the economic successes of Marxism. It is well worth reading again because everybody has forgotten that. Wilson said the Soviet Union was performing extremely well because it was not allowing the market to have its way – and this, he said, is what we ought to do. So even here an experiment was under way with state-based economic planning. And it didn't work.

What about your upbringing?

I was brought up in a very strong, loving home – my parents are still happily married. They thought that hard work and honesty were important virtues. We didn't have a car in the early years, or a television, but that didn't seem to matter. They moved into a home of their own for the first time when I was about five, and that was a really big step, in which we all took pride.

I won a scholarship to a direct-grant school at the age of ten. It was a Methodist foundation, so Methodist hymns and the King James Bible were very much a part of the rhythms of my early life. Religion is a part of my history and culture, something I share with most British people.

*Would you call yourself a Christian rather than some-
one who is committed to values, say, of decency and
integrity?*

Yes. I don't claim to be a faultless one by any means. I
go to church from time to time – not every Sunday, but
it's possible to have Christian beliefs without going to
an act of formal worship. There is the power of private
prayer, and the recognition in your daily life of Christian
obligations. I have Christian thoughts: I believe in God
and in the message of the New Testament.

The difference between a Christian and a non-Christian
is that a Christian believes that there is a higher authority
to whom you are answerable for your actions. It's quite
possible to develop an ethical system without believing in
God. People often mimic Christian standards and values.
They probably believe there was a figure called Christ,
and that he was a powerful preacher, but they don't
believe he was the Son of God. But they take a lot of
his principles and precepts, because, like me, they come
from a Christian culture.

*Do you think that the Church currently offers good
leadership to our society?*

I think there has been a failure of moral leadership all
too often. I made a statement when I was Secretary of
State for Wales that I thought more accent should be
placed on the Christian element of religious education in
Wales, particularly in primary schools, because Wales is
an almost entirely Christian culture – it doesn't have the
same concentration of other faiths that you find in some

140

of the big English cities. And the first people to condemn me were the Church leaders, who thought that even at an early stage religious education should be comparative and analytical and should not be primarily Christian in the way the 1944 Act says it should be.

But there are wider issues. I was involved in a debate in my own constituency with Church leaders. They had written to me, quite properly, complaining about the Government's housing policy: mainly they wanted more money spent on subsidised rented accommodation.

I asked them in turn whether they would make statements, in their pulpits and elsewhere, that it was better not to have children before you married and had a roof over your head. They were not prepared to say that: they couldn't understand the relevance of it. So I said, "Can't you see the problem? People are having babies at an earlier age, before they've settled down and have the financial wherewithal to support them. If you're really interested in the housing problem, you should be interested not only in whether there are enough houses but also when households are formed, whether it might not be better for people to wait a little longer and marry first and sort out their money a bit more."

Some of them were reluctant to see the problem in the round: that you had to look at the demand side of the situation as well as the Government's response on the supply side.

Belief in Politics

Is the Church failing to give a lead because it imagines its task is to adapt to a changing culture in the cause of relevance, rather than defending Christian tradition in the name of authority?

I think there is a danger of that. There is nothing wrong with the Church seeing its mission as being to help the dispossessed or the poor – it is a very important Christian precept. But when they think all the answers must come from the Government and none from the community itself, that's where I start to take issue with them. The message of the Bible is not only one of charity – and rightly so: if someone is disabled or really down on their luck, then of course we should help, either through our charity or more often through state provision – but also that you have a duty to yourself and your family to take responsibility where you can.

I think that side of the Christian message has sometimes got lost. I think that this is one of the reasons why the churches are emptying: the Church is alienating its traditional supporters, who believe both in charity and in taking responsibility, and it isn't winning those whose cause it is championing.

There has been a convergence recently in politics which makes it hard for many people to see any difference between the major parties. What has caused this?

I think there has been a blurring on a lot of the domestic issues because this Conservative administration has increased state spending quite substantially in recent years and Labour are now cutting back their plans to increase spending and tax because they see they were deeply unpopular.

Labour have accepted a lot of our measures. They won't reverse a lot of our privatisations. I think even Labour would accept that the privatisation of British Telecom was a success which has provided better service at a more realistic price – so much so that Mr Blair now wants to do deals with BT and seems to enjoy them being in the private sector. If you believe their words, I think Labour accept that there have to be limits to state borrowing and taxation and expenditure. So those are all advances that the Conservatives have made in the conduct of the economic debate. The main change has been in Labour.

The issue before the electorate at the next election will be: can you believe them? Won't they, under pressure of office, end up having to increase spending and taxation rather more than they say they would like? And will Tony Blair be able to keep control of his own party? We all know that Labour is by origin a high-tax, high-spend party. It was set up to take money away from those who had reasonable jobs and give it to those who didn't. If you believe in that, maybe you should do more of it rather than less.

What distinctive differences are there between the way you perceive the world and the way someone like Gordon Brown or Tony Blair does?

The principal differences are ones of degree. A good party politician shouldn't say that because the parties are always trying to show the electorate that they are

very different – though I think that is less true now
because Tony Blair is copying a lot of Conservative
principles.

First of all, what do we agree on? That democracy
is the best way (or the least bad way) of organising
government. That people should have a voice and a
vote. That the main purpose of government is to create
a climate or framework in which people can prosper
and be happy. That we would rather have a growing
economy than a shrinking one. We'd rather have more
people able to take care of their own families than
relying on the state. We'd rather have more people
in jobs.

That much is agreed. The disagreements are over how
you achieve that. We're really arguing about the right
balance between self-reliance and state dependency. At
the margins Conservatives would say: "People can do a bit
more for themselves. We can give them more opportunity;
we can encourage them to be more responsible." Labour
at the margins would say: "In order to avoid being
mean, you must extend state provision because that is
the charitable thing to do." That is really the centrepiece
of the debate.

There is now another crucial debate over identity,
which I hope will be important in the next election.
Do you think you're primarily British or primarily
European? Now, I'm European in the sense that Britain
is part of Europe geographically and part of its history
and culture. It will always play a very important part
in Europe and will always have big interests in it.
But when it comes to identity, I am British. I don't
belong to a European superstate and I don't feel any
loyalty to a place called Europe. I feel my loyalties

to a country called Britain, under one queen and one Parliament.

Labour, I think, no longer feel that very strongly. There are times when Mr Blair uses the language of patriotism, but when it comes to British institutions, everything is negotiable. On this issue I think there is a growing and important divide.

But isn't it true that a new political paradigm is emerging which focuses on community and on responsibilities rather than rights?

I don't know about paradigms. I don't think in those terms. I think in terms of what people want and the issues that are likely to ignite political controversy. I think there are going to be plenty of those. This idea that the passing of communism means the end of history is the biggest piece of nonsense I've read for a long time. In a way, history has broken out again: just go to Eastern Europe and you can see. Many of those conflicts and tensions have been in cold store for forty-five years because they had been suppressed by ruthless state power.

I think the big issues for this country in the Nineties and beyond are going to be constitutional issues – whether you need regional government, whether you need to surrender more power to the European institutions, whether you need a single currency and so forth – which go to the very heart of who you are and whether you're a nation or not. The battles over economic management are going to be less intense than they are now maybe.

But to what extent is the European discussion an economic discussion about the need to have an efficient common market and to what extent is it a political argument about sovereignty? The right has been saying for years, "Let the market decide." Isn't it the markets that actually undermine political authority?

I don't believe it's just about a common market or just about sovereignty. I think it is about identity. One of the most important passions of politics is: where do you feel you belong? Where do I feel my main loyalties lie? Those passions become very important, as we see in places like Yugoslavia and Northern Ireland, where they are the cause of conflict as well as political debate.

One of my objections to the extension of European institutional power is that it will take power away not just from Westminster but also from business, families, people themselves. I think government currently does too much, and therefore I oppose extensions of state power, from Brussels or Westminster. There are rather more of them at the moment coming from Brussels because you have a group of people who want more power, and the obvious thing to do is to take it away from people rather than from political institutions that are a bit better defended.

These arguments have gone well beyond questions of economic efficiency. We are now arguing about all the trappings of a state. Why does a common market need a flag, an anthem, a common army, a shared currency, a supreme court, a single central bank? You don't need any of those things to have a successful trading area: all you need to do is reduce the barriers to the free flow of goods and services.

146

John Redwood

Now, of course I agree that if people in the market decide to do things, that may well limit state power. That, I think, is a benefit in most cases. The state should only intervene and regulate the market where there is a clear abuse. For example, it should block or break up monopolies because they are against the public interest.

Every Christian has a moral obligation to look for the weaknesses in anything they espouse. You're an enthusiastic advocate of capitalism. What are its moral weaknesses?

I think there are two big problems which government has to address. The first relates to imperfections in the marketplace itself. There is in business a tendency towards cartel or monopoly if unchecked. The machine can only deliver prosperity and freedom if monopoly and cartel are stopped, by government action if necessary. So I am a strong believer in a very firm competition policy. You need to stop unreasonable mergers. Often it's agreed mergers that are the most dangerous because they will be the ones that provide the conspiracy against the public, and you need to be vigilant about cartels and price rings because that is the power of business exploiting the customer.

That's why the water industry is currently unsatisfactory. It's slightly better than being a state monopoly because state monopolies are nearly always evil as far as the customer is concerned. It's none the less not delivering the quality of service at the price that should be delivered. The only answer to that is to introduce

147

real competition so that the customer's interest can be better served.

The other problem is that there will be, at any one time, a number, maybe a significant number, of people who cannot provide for their needs and wants through the market because they are disabled or elderly or frail or cannot compete for one reason or another. Conservatives have always accepted that you should levy taxation on the strong and successful in order to make some money available to those who otherwise would not have sufficient.

The argument in politics is about getting the balance right. Are you identifying those who are in real need, who genuinely can't find something to help themselves, and are you still leaving enough incentive so that it is always worth while working and taking responsibility if you can? Those are sensitive issues. You can get so far in defining general rules – very often you have to make judgments by individual cases.

Is not one weakness of the market that it gives freedom of choice to people who may choose evil?

Well, you limit their capacity to choose evil by law. You can't have free enterprise, or capitalism as you put it, unless you have a strong law of contract and relatively safe streets. If free trade is always going to be interrupted by burglary or violence, if customers are going to be exploited by business people who effectively carry out criminal acts at their expense, then you can't have a proper or successful trade. So you do need a strong state who will say, "This goes beyond normal,

reasonable contract." For example, financial services
are now a very important part of the economy. It is
not up to the state to say, "You shouldn't buy these
things; you should buy those," because it has no more
knowledge, and probably less, than anyone else of what's
going to go up or down. You have to take your own
risks in making investments, and you take advice. But
if somebody comes into the marketplace and says, "I
will take your savings and invest them in government
securities," and then he puts your money in a Swiss bank
account in his own name and disappears, that is an act of
theft and something the state should be trying to prevent
by law.

There are criminal tendencies in state enterprise as
well: it is not a prerogative of capitalism to breed
crooks and a prerogative of Marxism to breed honest
men. The levels of venality and corruption in many
communist states have been quite shocking – usually
worse than the levels of criminality in free-enterprise
societies.

*Is there not a tendency in free enterprise to reduce things
to the lowest moral common denominator? Look at the
entertainment industry.*

If you want a free and a moral society – and I think
the two are inextricably linked – you must rely on the
judgment and good taste of the public. Law-makers can
sometimes influence or lead, but sometimes they are
just reflecting the way social mores are moving. But I
would take issue with you if you think it's a necessary
attribute of free enterprise and not of state control. There

is no guarantee that a state-run system will have better standards. Just look at some of the scandals we've had in local government: you can't say they've always met the highest ethical standards in the way they have conducted themselves in the area of care in children's homes, for example.

How do you account for the present cynicism in our society, which not only ridicules our leaders but often seems determined to pull them down?

In part it's healthy. One of the prices of living in a free society as a political leader or thinker is that you will be satirised and attacked. Some people say, "This Government is being undermined by some very nasty cartoonists," but the cartoons of the eighteenth century were far worse, often satirising politicians of enormous stature. Their image has survived what were lethal attacks at the time.

The second issue you raise is being pulled off the pedestal. It's dangerous to put yourself on too tall a pedestal to start with because it then becomes irresistible for people to pull you down. It's very important that political leaders should only support causes or back principles that they believe they are living up to themselves. There is a danger for any leader, if he makes a statement about how others should live, if he is not himself living up to that standard – which is why many politicians think it's always wrong to offer strong moral leadership in politics because you are subject to counter-attack. The press will obviously take delight in revealing humbug.

The younger generation seems to be less interested in national politics than any previous generation – the statistics for voter registration among eighteen- to thirty-four-year-olds are quite dismal. What do you attribute that to, and what do we do about it?

If I do have a criticism of modern politics, I suppose it is that at the moment there aren't enough people putting forward a vision of why living in a free society, a nation with a proud tradition, with clear cultural and constitutional underpinnings, is something to celebrate. Politicians have to offer visions of the future that appeal to younger as well as older people. Each generation has a precious inheritance in this country, but it also has its own contribution to make, and I think it's up to us, the political leaders, to get that across to the whole country and to get more enthusiasm for politics.

You are right about voting tendencies, but I find, travelling the country and speaking to student audiences as I often do, there's still a lot of excitement about and interest in the business of politics. Young people are interested in debating the real issues. They sometimes think that politicians as a whole are somehow trying to walk away from them.

It's regrettable that politics has changed so much, but perhaps inevitable. People mainly see their politicians on television, in the same way as they see media stars, rather than having lots of opportunities for big public meetings and heckling and all the things that brought politics to life in the nineteenth and early twentieth centuries. It is so difficult for the public to actually read what the politician is saying. They read interpretations of it, which are often very different from what he has actually said, and they find them rather bizarre because very often they don't make a lot of sense. If you get the chance to meet them, you say, "Of course that's nonsense – *this* is what I said," and they see the point. But you can only see so many people like that, whereas millions see the other version. I think it creates barriers between the politician and his or her audience that they tend to see only what the media want them to see.

Do people have a clear idea of what you yourself are saying?

Well, it's up to me to get my message across. I'm not blaming the media in any way. I think people understand that I don't want a single currency and I think defending Britain and her institutions is important. I think they understand that I think there have been too many hospital closures. I think they understand that I think we could take £5,000 million off public spending next year without sacking a single nurse, teacher, doctor or policeman.

I don't think I've had quite so much good fortune explaining my views on the family. As soon as you say anything about the family, people like to twist and sensationalise it to make it more interesting from their point of view. That becomes a barrier to effective communication and decent discussion rather than a help. But that's life: I'm not complaining. I'll have another go.

What do you attribute the breakdown of the family to?

It's difficult to come up with any general answer. I've asked a lot of people because it's one of the most worrying features of our society. A number of my colleagues in the House who represent poorer constituencies say it is a lack of money which is breaking up the family. My constituents are more likely to tell me that they are both working too hard and too long to earn all the money they think they need for their agreed lifestyle. There are no obvious answers.

Some of the pressures to keep marriages together, or to form a marriage in the first place, have gone. Society doesn't seem to rate marriage as highly as it did twenty or thirty years ago. Some people say this is liberation because you shouldn't be held in a marriage that's unpleasant. Others say it's a great tragedy.

I think where young children are involved it is usually better to try and keep the marriage together. It is better to have two parents than one looking after a child. I think it's better for the parents too because even if the husband or the wife is very busy and can only be there a bit of the time, two pairs of hands and two pairs of eyes are better than one. Just being given the afternoon off to go and do something for yourself can be very important to a loving parent who would have to face the responsibilities of parenthood twenty-four hours a day, seven days a week, if they were on their own.

One last question: do you still aspire to the leadership of the Conservative Party?

I've always made it clear that I will only apply if there's a vacancy.

Biography

John Redwood was born in 1951 and was educated at Kent College, Canterbury, and Magdalen College, Oxford. He was elected a Fellow of All Souls College, Oxford, where he wrote a history of English thought in the seventeenth and eighteenth centuries.

Subsequently, he worked as an investment director with N. M. Rothschild, and as head of Rothschild's privatisation unit. From 1983 to 1985 he was head of Margaret Thatcher's Policy Unit at Number Ten, Downing Street. He became known as a powerful advocate for privatisation, private enterprise and global free trade.

He became Member of Parliament for Wokingham in the general election of 1987. In 1989 he joined the Government as a junior minister in the Department of Trade and Industry. In 1992 he was appointed Minister of State for Local Government and Inner Cities in the Department of the Environment. In 1993 he was appointed to the Cabinet as Secretary of State for Wales.

In June 1995 he resigned from the Cabinet in order to mount a campaign for the leadership of the Conservative Party; his attempt was unsuccessful.

He has written a number of books, including *Popular Capitalism* (1988), *The Global Marketplace, Capitalism and its Future* (1993) and *Public Enterprise in Crisis* (1980), in which he argues for deregulation and wider ownership as the basis of a prosperous and stable democratic order.

This interview was conducted on 7 November 1995.

Clare Short

Some people, looking at the moral passion evident in your politics, might say, "Whether she likes it or not, this woman is a Christian."

Well, I would feel honoured by that. But I'm not. I'm deeply influenced by my Catholic childhood, but I'm not a Christian. It's my Church, I understand it, I know it, I love it, it irritates me, but I've left it.

Sometimes I give my mum a lift to church at the weekend, and I think how fine and good it is. And I think I miss that. When you see the immigrant communities that came to Birmingham and their struggle to rebuild their religious institutions so that they can mark the great passages of life, the birth of children, the marriages and the deaths, there's something very fine about that. If I was creating social structures, I would say that Churches nurture the best in people, and we need them. If I had children I'd send them to Catholic schools. So that's a contradiction in my life.

I would have to be dishonest to pretend that I believe in a personal God. It's because I like him that I don't believe in him. If he existed, he wouldn't have made the world like this. He couldn't have because it isn't fair. It's fair that people should have challenges in life and have to make moral decisions and take responsibility for

155

themselves, of course, but you'd have to give everyone a fair crack, and the way the world is organised does not do that. Millions of children never have a life.

But I think God is the quest for goodness in humanity, and that's a very fine thing. Being decent includes being angry with evil and the hurt of people that is just not necessary.

Do you think then that the secularisation of our society has damaged us?

I think we are living through a pretty ugly phase of human civilisation, when we have worshipped money in a most crass and belittling way. I don't yearn for an earlier time because then people obeyed rather than necessarily believed. A lot of people would have just been bending their knee because they had to.

But I think we are lacking a moral space in our public discourse; I tend to use the word "moral" rather than "spiritual". Maybe it will come back. I think people across the world think that things are very ugly. It connects with all this current sleaze stuff. People don't want to be sanctimonious, but I think most people want to belong to a community that seeks to be decent.

Can pluralism be an oppressive thing because nobody is allowed to say that their own values are universal in case they offend someone?

Pluralism includes accommodating those who want to convert everybody to something. It has to, by definition. I think it might be the case that the break-up of the old certainties has partly generated this confusion. People feel uncomfortable talking about their fundamental beliefs and think that people will accuse them of seeking to impose them on others. But I don't think that is necessary. When you know what you believe you can be more understanding of others with passionate beliefs.

Fear of offence is less than real respect for your brother or sister of a different faith. It's based on ignorance. When we have properly grown up and we properly know and respect each other, people will talk easily about the differences in their beliefs.

Has the vacuum left by the role of religion in public life been filled by economics? People now get their security and identity from the things they own.

The thing about money is it is desperately important if you haven't got a job or if you are struggling with the basics – overwhelmingly important. But once you have those, it has no meaning. It gives nothing to the human spirit to have six houses and ten cars. The most profound things about being human are not to do with money. We need something beyond our own selfishness.

Tax cuts for those who have already got plenty, when we've got all this pain in our society, are immoral, an appeal to greed. Our politics is pivoting around an immorality, and it appears to work. But I think politicians deeply underestimate the decency of people. They think their motives are much more base than they actually are. How you distribute the economic wealth of a country is a profoundly moral question. I think that talking only about the economy is part of this loss of moral discourse.

157

But it isn't just the economy. People care about their
families, and so politicians start talking about families,
and then, because they haven't got a generous way of
talking, they fall into problems like "Back to Basics"
and their own double standards. But I feel that people
want politicians to offer support even if they disagree
with them. People despise this discourse we're in at the
moment. It isn't just the sleaze; it is that no one will raise
the standards of the debate to something higher, about
justice and morality and fairness.

At university I did political science, as they call it, and
I did a lot of political and moral philosophy. "What is
good?", "What is just?" and "How do we know?" have
always been dominant questions for me. My politics is
all part of that quest and that journey from my Catholic
childhood.

The ideas of socialism come from a moral vision. The
left has a tradition of moral protest, but there is a caution
about talking that language now because we have been
battered down by past failure. There's a suspicion that
this low-level politics of tax cuts works and therefore we
can't risk something finer. I can't speak for others, but I
feel that's what's going on. But people are yearning for
something more honest. That's my intuition.

*The Christian roots of socialism have re-emerged with
leaders like John Smith and Tony Blair. Has that affected
the way Labour presents itself to the country?*

I don't know. The danger would be that Christianity
comes back into fashion and then everyone has to pretend
to be a Christian, and that is not honest. I hate that kind

of thing. There are lots of people who pose as Christians who I don't think are.

The Christians are absolutely entitled to be proud of their beliefs, but they have to show respect for people of other beliefs. John was good at it because he was so clear about who he was. His Christianity was a deep part of what he was, but he wasn't a Holy Joe; he liked fun. Tony is newer, obviously, and we will see how he handles it. But his Christianity is completely sincere and part of his life.

Why do we have so little respect for politicians? We seem nowadays to make a distinction between legal power, which they have, and moral authority, which we think they lack.

I know what you mean. I sometimes hear my colleagues talking as though politics is something politicians do to people, whereas it isn't. People put politicians in place, through elections, to make the changes they voted for that enable them to do things with their lives. That's really how it works.

Society has always had a disrespect for politicians, but I think it is at an all-time low. I think there is derision. People despise all the noise and stupidity. And politicians have lost authority because they have been hopeless. They haven't delivered the goods and they are seen to be putting their hands in the till too much and looking after themselves while others suffer. It's very dangerous. If people get very cynical about politics and politicians get very cautious about saying anything can be done, people give up on democracy and on the sense that together we can improve our society.

But it is not just Britain: it's going on everywhere. I think another factor at work is the globalisation of capital and the nation-state's loss of control over some very important economic and moral concerns. The figures on the multinationals are fantastic. Five hundred companies control 70 per cent of world trade, 30 per cent of the world's GDP and 80 per cent of foreign investment. So you've got a lot of politicians strutting around their national stages, pretending they can do something about it, and they can't.

What we have to do is look more clearly at where economic power lies and how we build human institutions to control that power for the benefit of the whole of humanity. I think that is what the battle over Europe is about in the Tory Party. Is it just a free market or do we have some minimum standards for people? Then people are starting to say there should be environmental standards in the GATT [General Agreement on Tariffs and Trades] and maybe a social chapter. I think this is where the future is.

There is nothing immoral about markets, and, as Gorbachev said, the market is as old as humanity. But capital is just money and it must be controlled. At the moment it is out of control. The forces of the free movement of capital and the free market are hurting people and de-developing the poorest countries. Big chunks of Africa are imploding. We are not using our knowledge, our ability and our wealth to give a decent minimum to the people of the world, and we could do it. Hunger is not necessary, and this is an absolute moral failure.

Clare Short

But is there any individual in the world who can actually say "No" when the markets say "Yes"?

People said nothing could be done about the recession in the Thirties, which spread poverty all over the world. And we got a new political settlement because there were people like Keynes, with big ideas, who faced up to a worldwide economic failure and set up new international institutions which gave us for fifty years a more generous and civilised world.

Now there are changes that mean we need a new settlement. The whole fashion of monetarism has just let the market rip, and it is ripping away at the most basic decencies of human life in both rich and poor countries. We need not just another leader but a surge of ideas and then the political will to implement them. That is overdue but it will come, I think.

I don't fully understand how inflation became such a beast that it had to be attacked at such incredible cost across the world. Obviously, it is very inconvenient if prices keep going up, but I'd much rather live with that than with spreading hunger and homelessness and famine in Africa. I'm not saying that it is one or the other, but I think that inflation is a funny thing to set up as the biggest evil of our time.

The monetarists said that if we just obey their theory, the world will be perfect. It bloody isn't. We said it was unacceptable to run society by increasing inequality, and they said, "Ha,ha, we'll produce more and it will trickle down." Now we know it is not only morally repugnant, it doesn't work. Thank heavens – it would have been a moral conundrum for us if it did.

The nub of the question is: is an economic theory that is

161

content with gross inequality morally acceptable? I think it is not. I think the moral argument has been obscured by a language of economics that most people don't have access to, so they can't enter the debate and they are all pushed to one side.

Don't you think that justice and freedom can only be reconciled in a religious world view? In a rational, secular politics they become separate and often opposed. The left has championed one and the right has championed the other.

I don't agree. I think the differences between the left and the right are much more complex now, both within and between parties. But I think historically the right has represented the interests of wealth and business and the left has represented the ordinary people, and that was the conflict. Of course, there are moral people in the world of business, but I suppose I have seen that morality was on our side because we represented the poor and the ordinary people who wanted a fairer world. But increasingly, as the Tory Party becomes not conservative but bigotedly right-wing, I see that there was once a moral Conservatism. It was paternalistic, but it was a world view that said everyone had to be included and cared for. But a more vicious right has emerged in recent years that says inequality is good for everyone, including the poor, because in the end you will get a better economy and somehow they will benefit.

I think we are probably moving to a new thesis, when the crudity of those two divided interests won't do any more and we have got to pull them together. But I don't agree at all that the right has been for freedom and the left has been for justice. Who fought for democracy, for equal rights? It was the dispossessed, the poor. It is those who have nothing who need democracy and freedom and a voice to gain a more just order. They go together. You can't have one without the other. I think you are profoundly wrong to see them as antagonistic. It would be deeply depressing if you were right.

One difference between the left and the right, surely, is that the left would say that freedom of choice means nothing unless you first have the power to choose. If I see a hundred goodies in the shop window but I don't have the means to buy them, I am not free to choose.

Absolutely. The UN Declaration on Human Rights says that everyone has a right to life and to education. If you don't have a social settlement that allows everyone to be human, it is a disgusting and immoral settlement. A lot of the ideas of the hard right are immoral. But we have lived through a period when they were celebrated as economically necessary and therefore people weren't allowed to debate whether it was a moral choice, which it was. You see the frailty of the human intellect. We think we're so clever, but the big questions go unasked.

It is not true that the poor of Africa and the dispossessed of Europe are in competition. If everyone is given the chance to work and consume the basic decencies of life, then everyone will have to start working harder because there are a lot of people not getting the basics.

You use very strong language. Do you recognise that there are moral evils lurking in your own vision of a decent, just society?

I admit that in the big ideas of the left there have been repression and misuse of power in the name of being fair. We have seen all the tyranny and the lies and the cruelty in the Soviet Union. I think it is deeply unfair to blame Marx for that; nothing he wrote justified what went on there and he would have abominated that ugly, brutal, evil regime. Lenin can be partly blamed, though, of course, he was a revolutionary leader, and things that were legitimate in the overthrow of a very old, corrupt settlement are not legitimate when you're running a country. The social democratic parties have never supported the communists because we have always said that democracy is intrinsic to our value system.

One of the reasons, I think, why the left has been weakened internationally is that ordinary, sensible people see what went on in the Soviet Union and think, "Do they believe in that?" But most people in the Labour Party, if they had lived in the Soviet Union, would have been in the Gulag. I think the people who would have been in the Communist Party, with all their privileged access to goods, maybe sit on the other side of the House.

Are you saying you're a social democrat, not a socialist, after all? A pragmatist rather than an idealist?

I'm a socialist. But it's just language, and language is used differently in different countries.

Since I gave up on Catholicism, I've poured most of my passionate moral searching into my socialism. And in a funny way, I suppose, into the Labour Party, though it is not a satisfactory Church. I think that being a politician is quite like being a priest. You try to live by what you say you believe, and you work hard to get the outcomes people want from the office you hold.

But you've never held office. Do you feel you have served the people you represent, many of whom are very poor, better by being an idealist than a pragmatist willing to compromise?

I've been an MP for eleven years, and I suppose when I started out I thought I would just speak up for those values and those people and their rights and it would happen. But I have been part of the failure of my party and its ideas to win elections and then change the social order in a way that would benefit the kind of people who vote for me and celebrate the values I believe in. Socialism is a beautiful moral vision, but it hasn't done very well in the real world lately. It has let people down very badly.

I feel now that I must use whatever influence I have to try to win the next election and deliver some social reform because people are hurting and they need a sense that things can be better. If this doesn't happen next time, my political life will have been a failure, and in a sense my moral journey will have been a failure. It doesn't mean my believing will ever be wrong, but I will have failed in my major life work. But say we failed again, though I don't think we will. Just to speak up for the truth and for better values is still a worthwhile thing to do.

Do you approve of the way the Churches have spoken out on political issues?

I welcome it, but I think they have been too polite, too conventional. Send a few postcards and tell the politicians what they think, and the politicians just ignore them. The lobbying has been for the right causes, but it should have been more angry and righteous, and they should have meant it more.

It's funny. This period of ugliness has renewed lots of forces for good. Good can come out of evil, and the recommitment of the Churches to work for justice and to care for people, and to cooperate with different faiths is a good reaction to it.

Clearly you differ over some of the fundamental issues. A lot of Catholics think passionately that abortion is a monstrous and evil thing, but I'm sure it is a minority who think it should be illegal. In a perfect world there would never be abortion, but there will never be a perfect world. It is different, you know, when you are a woman: you just know that sometimes it is the moral thing to do. I once had a letter from a woman, maybe in her sixties, who had been raped as a young woman and had a daughter whom she always hated. I think that is a tragedy.

We still have far too many late abortions and unnecessary abortions because we are not very sorted out on sex education for young people. We think it is moral to tell them nothing. Abortion is always regrettable.

A lot of the Church's concern has been about the breakdown of social morals since the Sixties. Do you sympathise with that perception?

I do think that in terms of economic crime there has been a moral breakdown. I remember my childhood – I grew up in my constituency – we once had a burglary in our house and the whole street talked about it for months. Now there are lots of young males with nothing to do, and it is true the Devil makes work for idle hands. Also we have far more material things. There wasn't so much to burgle before.

But in terms of sex and so on, I think there was gross hypocrisy before, and the Sixties were partly about being more honest about all that. There is a myth of the happy family and the permanent marriage, that it was all orderly and decent; but I think there were lots of hidden cruelties: prostitution, incredible violence against wives. Look at child abuse. Sexual abuse of children is an enormously painful, unimaginable thing, but I think the evidence is absolutely clear that it has been going on for hundreds of years. It was hidden: no one even talked about it. And that was a more cruel and evil society than this, now that we admit it.

Of course, it would be wonderful if every sexual relationship was completely happy and tender and caring, but we're a long way from that. And to pretend that it used to be is a lie. There is a long way to go to make things really decent, but I think we are making progress, not going backwards.

Your party is talking about the need to revive a sense of community. But we have become a nation of individuals in our semi-detached houses and our private cars. How are we going to rebuild a fragmented society?

Being with the people you like spending time with is one of the things human beings are entitled to. No one has a duty to mix all their lives with people they don't particularly like. But there are parts of their life – going to school, going shopping, going to the local park – that require them to cooperate with others to share the goodness of life. The only way they can secure it for themselves is to secure it for others.

I think things are more individualised. But even if you are a multi-millionaire and you live in Los Angeles, the riots erupt around you too. Your children have to go to school, even if you pay for it, and mix with other children. You are going to get sick, and you will be old yourself one day. There's no way people can opt out of society. They might pretend to themselves in good times that they can, but it is unsustainable as a way for a lot of human beings to live on a shared piece of earth.

This is all enlightened self-interest. Is there anything you can appeal to, since God is out of the picture, to encourage people to rise above their own interest?

I don't think this is hard if we say to each other it is our duty as human beings to work for a society where we as individuals can have a decent life and so can our neighbours. If you are saying that if we don't have a personal God, there is no morality, I just don't agree. Being moral is intrinsic to being human.

The concept of sin is a brilliant part of Christian teaching – that we all have to try to be good, but we fail. People can do great evil, but we know it is wrong and we usually regret it, and we can be sorry and we can be forgiven. No one's a write-off. I visited Winson Green Prison recently and talked to the prisoners. They are real, complete human beings. A lot of them have not had educational opportunities, and they were looking for a future that didn't include crime.

I think the Christian teaching that you must love your neighbour as yourself is a description of what humans are like. Most humans do care about other people; they don't like to see distress. Most people hate the fact that we have got beggars. They are scared of them and embarrassed, but they don't want to live in a society where some people have got nowhere to live.

Many people belong to community groups and associations. There are tenants' groups and residents' groups, and people are getting on with it: not all but many, of all religions and none. And most people see the people who do that as good. It is part of being human to think that people who help others are good.

It has not been celebrated and honoured in our political discourse. We have lived through a period when public service has been demeaned and only the yuppies in the City were clever. All those values of selfishness and greed were disseminated from the highest levels of the society, by government, by the respectable newspapers and so on. It has been a bad time, and a very disappointing time, but I think something better is coming.

Biography

Clare Short was born in Birmingham in 1946 and educated locally at St Paul's Grammar School. She graduated from Leeds University with a BA in Political Science.

Between 1970 and 1975 she worked as a civil servant in the Home Office. She was then director of All Faiths for One Race from 1976 to 1978 and director of YouthAid from 1979 to 1983.

A member of the Labour Party since 1970, she was elected MP for Ladywood, Birmingham, in 1983.

Between 1985 and 1986 she chaired an all-party parliamentary group on race relations. She became a member of the National Executive Committee of the Labour Party in 1988; the vice-president of Socialist International Women in 1992; and chair of the National Executive Committee's Women's Committee in 1993.

She has been the Labour Party's spokesperson on employment, 1985 to 1989; on social security, 1989 to 1991; on environmental protection, 1992 to 1993; and on women, 1993 to 1995.

She was elected to the shadow Cabinet in 1995 and is currently shadow Secretary of State for Transport.

Her second husband, Alex Lyon, who was a former Labour MP for York, died in 1993.

Two interviews were conducted with Clare Short on 24 November 1994 and 24 October 1995.

Jack Straw

What values did your upbringing instil in you?

I was brought up in the Congregational Church. My parents were pacifists; my father had been a conscientious objector during the war and went to prison for that. My maternal grandfather had been a very strong trade unionist. He'd been a shop steward at the bus garage at Loughton. He used to hold me spellbound with stories about how his forebears had fought the lords of the manor to prevent them enclosing Epping Forest in the middle of the last century.

Sadly, my parents broke up. I got a boarding scholarship to Brentwood School, which had a strong Anglican tradition. I was in the school choir, and so I went to chapel seven or eight times a week and got to know the Prayer Book backwards. In the late Eighties I began to think much more actively about my Christian faith, and I was confirmed in 1989.

There wasn't any shaft of light or anything: I suppose it gradually crept up on me. What drew me back to the Church was the power of the Christian message and the stunning example of Christ and his utterly remarkable insights into human emotional behaviour. Those insights are timeless: that's what I think is so extraordinary about him.

171

Belief in Politics

Our culture is increasingly pluralist and increasingly secular. Do you think that has damaged our society or set us adrift?

I don't remotely suggest that those who don't go to church don't have a framework of belief, and I don't regret the rise of pluralism. I think it is a natural concomitant of a democratic society. When we stopped burning dissenters at the stake, that inevitably led to people challenging the whole basis of Christianity. That's fine. I don't regret that at all. I do regret the amorality of much of our modern culture, which I think is best illustrated by much of the content of the tabloid press, and much of what I see on television, which doesn't seem to me to have much of a moral framework.

That's not taking a high horse: I am very clear that what people do in their private lives is very much a matter for them. I think it's for those without sin to cast the first stone, and I'm certainly not in that category. But the gratuitous violence on television, the utter obsession of the tabloid press with sexual matters and the intrusion into people's private misery I find depressing.

Politicians get pretty short shrift from the tabloids, don't they?

Certainly the press constantly suggests that anybody in a leadership position has feet of clay. What I think has happened is this: as the ideological divide in politics has changed, there has been an even sharper focus on individual politicians. Leaders are put on pedestals and then the press tries to knock them down.

172

It's right that people should be sceptical about politicians because anybody with power should have that power challenged, but this is different. It contributes to an enormous cynicism about the political process which is very, very corrosive. Personally, it puts iron in my soul. I am damned if I am going to be defeated by it.

Given all the pressure and stress, why are you in politics?

I have always wanted to be: I articulated an ambition to be a Member of Parliament when I was thirteen. How precocious can you get!

I've never wanted to be a time-server: I'm in politics to achieve things. I'm fascinated by ideas and by their power, and the power of the word. The opening of St John's Gospel says: "In the beginning was the Word, and the Word was with God and the Word was God," but the Greek word *logos* can also mean "idea".

You were the author of a pamphlet advocating a replacement for Clause IV, which defines the priorities of the Labour Party. Isn't it all apple pie and motherhood? What is there in it that the Conservatives would disagree with?

If a Tory ideologue had to write what the Tory Party stood for, one or two of the words would be the same, but I think the overriding sense would be very different. They would sign up to freedom of choice and opportunity, but in different contexts. Modern Tories on the whole don't talk about fairness, but one of the reasons I put freedom of choice and opportunity in is because the Tories have tried to copyright them, and I believe there are greater freedoms, choices and opportunities to be offered by a democratic socialist route than a Tory route. Let's look at my suggestions and see what the Tories would make of them.

"The power of the community is used to advance the interests of the individual and the family and the individual liberty is enhanced by collective provision." Modern Tories wouldn't use that formulation. They are much more individualistic: the right-wing, who are dominant, have a concept of family but not of society.

". . . where religious, racial, sexual equality is guaranteed." I don't think any Tory would use that formulation. They would think it was dangerous and would draw them down the road of quotas and targets and things like that.

Some Tories would agree with "equality of opportunity"; few, I think, would subscribe to "greater equity in the distribution of life's rewards". They make a case for inequity; they say this is the way you get a dynamic market economy.

"Markets should be the servants not the masters of the community." Many of them would say you can't achieve that. "To these ends the community should intervene through appropriate measures of regulation and control and public ownership." They certainly wouldn't have the last. "Labour wants and works for a world in which poverty, deprivation, injustice and oppression are eliminated." They wouldn't put that in that way, given their record on human rights.

174

Jack Straw

I take it for granted that you think the Tory vision of the world is mistaken, but do you think it is actually immoral?

I don't think there's something immoral about the whole party: that would be a very arrogant assertion. I think there is something lacking in the morality of the right wing of the party.

These days the major fault-line in politics lies about a third of the way across the Tory Party. The basic difference is between those who are committed to civic society, who see that societies can only operate if there is an ethical framework which can't be provided by the market, and those on the right wing, or part of the right wing, of the Tory Party who believe that all social relations can be dictated by the market and it's just too bad if some people fall by the wayside.

How does "new" Labour differ from "old" Labour? In its ends or its means?

Both. Some people wanted an end to private property: that was certainly a very powerful idea at the time when the old Clause IV was written and right through the Thirties. I think that confusion was something which hobbled us. Now there is a greater clarity about our goal, which is to produce a fairer society in which people find greater satisfaction in being members of a community and the reciprocity which that brings.

We're not offering people something which is abstract, but something they can feel. I think people know what a functional community is: it's one where people can look each other in the eyes, where calling someone a stranger is a mark of affection not of fear. I think travel makes a big difference because people know when they're in a community where they feel comfortable and they can work out, maybe in a rather inchoate way, why that is.

We have changed some of the means. One of Tony Blair's great merits is that he has raised the issue of ethics in politics to a much greater extent than his predecessors. He took the great risk that he might sound prudish or hectoring, but he's achieved it without, I think, too much criticism.

There has to be a moral basis to politics. There has to be an element of trust in a democratic system. Unless people have a reasonable certainty that what you say you'll do is what you will do, the whole process falls apart.

But can Labour do what it says it will do? You are under pressure all the time to cost your promises.

And we are also always being enticed to say we'll put everything back to where it was. We can't do that because, if we do, we won't be able to deliver what we are promising, and that's why our caution is fully consistent with what I hope is a more straightforward, ethical approach to politics.

I think people understand that. They are not stupid. There is this awful assumption by some people in politics that the public are there to be hoodwinked.

We hear a lot about the resurgence of Christian Socialism.

Is that genuine? Many Christians still see Labour as anti-Christian in its stance on abortion, say.

I've got to pick my words with care here. I don't believe that the issue of abortion is particularly illuminated by reference to Christian theology. There are plenty of active Christians who support choice; others are opposed to all abortion. But you would have to take a very sectarian view of Christianity to suggest that a party must be opposed to Christianity because it is, generally speaking, in favour of a right to abortion. I will continue to vote in favour of the right of women to have an abortion in properly controlled circumstances.

Yes, Christian Socialism is very vibrant in the party. I think it has become more vibrant, actually, and more self-confident since the collapse of communism because there is no longer a tension between a Marxist draw and a Christian draw. A very large part of Labour's moral basis is drawn from its Christian roots. That's not to say the party is a Christian Socialist party – we have people of varying religious persuasions and none, especially these days – but non-conformist Christianity has been hugely important in the Labour Party.

Do you think it's misleading that so much of the analysis of what is wrong with our society is expressed in terms of economics?

I think the most obvious indicator of a fractured society is economic, the fact that some people are very rich and some are very poor. It is that which most detaches people from society. So you can't get away from economics. But I've never thought that's enough. You can't just create a political programme on the basis of an economic one. Indeed, how do you make your judgments about distribution except within some broader moral framework?

I think it's still important that we talk about the economic consequences of government, because I don't see how you can get away from them. But certainly the Labour Party has shifted remarkably over the last ten years from the time when our answer to everything was that we should spend more money on it. We aren't going to have that much money to spend on things anyway.

So how does a Labour Government change society without spending more money?

Partly it's where you spend existing budgets. Take the transport system. There's still a large amount of money being spent on the roads. Now, we may need to continue to spend a large amount on roads, but you can at least make a decision about whether you're spending on road systems or public transport systems. I happen to think that public transport systems are very important for the functioning of communities because they're things which people can share. London would be impoverished without buses – I really mean that. People feel safe travelling on buses, particularly crewed buses. And on the top of a 159 bus you meet people you wouldn't otherwise meet, which I think is important.

Does that mean that all politicians should travel by bus?

It must be a matter of personal choice, but I enjoy using London's buses.

There are plenty of things a Government can do which are not directly related to cash. The cost of changing the constitution of the country is tiny in global terms; it's just administration. But the dividends would be huge if we get it right. If we have our Freedom of Information Act, our own Bill of Rights, if we sign up to the European Convention on Human Rights, if we have a referendum on voting systems, if we change the House of Lords, have devolution to Scotland and Wales and give English regions their own voice, these things could make a really big difference, if they're presented properly, and they would cost very little.

In education, money needs to be spent, but one of the reasons morale is so low is because county schools see money going to grant-maintained schools. That seems unfair, and it is.

So I'm reasonably sanguine about all this. In any event, I think if we pretend that the only route to political success is by spending more money, we're almost bound to fail.

You talk of the benefits of reforming our democracy, but a growing number of people seem not to care about it. A recent survey for the think-tank Demos* found that the

* Helen Wilkinson and Geoff Mulgan, *Freedom's Children: Work, Relationships and Politics for 18–34-year-olds in Britain Today*, Demos, London, 1995.

179

younger generation is four times less likely than their predecessors even to register to vote.

I think they do care about it, but they feel detached from it. A lot of these people are involved in single-issue politics. One of the ironies of that is that it's all directed to persuading old-style, middle-aged politicians to change their minds. There's nothing that single-issue groups can do by themselves. We need to say to people that single-issue politics is a dead end by itself. Also it can too often lead to single-answer politics: the suggestion that there's only ever one answer to some very complicated questions.

We also need to give people a better sense that society is committed to them. I think we are seeing in Europe and elsewhere a huge reaction to the global village. People want some sort of tribal identity, some sense of belonging and of a shared culture. Sometimes it is expressed in horrific terms, as in Bosnia or Chechenya; but it is terribly important. Politicians ignore that at their peril.

But the same report found that 24 per cent of eighteen- to thirty-four-year-olds take pride in being outside the system of institutions and traditions. It calls them "the underwolves" because they are going to bite back. These people don't know what a community looks like.

I think they are part of their own community. When I witnessed people being brought down from tree-houses in the line of a motorway to my constituency I was struck by their sense of cohesion. Because they are the underdogs, they've experienced being part of a wider family.

But providing those people with the opportunity of work and with dignity in society is one of the biggest challenges we face. You've got to tackle homelessness and long-term unemployment, particularly among the young. There are problems of education and training for some of them, though by no means for all. And for some people who are on the streets there are problems of mental illness and maybe addiction as well.

Having tackled all those things, you can then say, "We need something in return from you, not in terms of your private lives but your behaviour in public." Some of them can be very intimidating and we don't think that's in order. I'm very much in favour of rights, but one man's or woman's right is someone else's responsibility. You can't simply say, "You have a right to this, a right to that, a right to something else," without saying, "Hang on! You've also got obligations." We've got to rebuild this idea of responsibilities.

It's going to take time, I think. People do change as they get older. What's attractive when you are twenty-four is very unattractive when you are thirty-four. Some will stay with an alternative lifestyle, but I suspect that an awful lot may react against it. People said that the Sixties were going to lead to communism and generations of hippy children and grandchildren, but they didn't.

Then we need to break the cycle of bad parenting. It must be true that how people are parented has a profound effect on how they relate to everybody else: I think we can at least glean that from 150 years of psychology. Parenting is of huge importance and we need to make it a public issue.

How can you do that without appearing to intrude into people's private lives?

I'm having a lot of conversations with people, and I'm trying to work out how you do it in a way that, first, does not appear to be seeking party advantage and, second, makes people sit up without making them think, "Why is that person telling me how to bring up my kids?" The advantage of being a politician is that you can get a hearing for things. You can sometimes just crack open an issue in a way that others can't. But you have to inject a bit of humility into this, and make sure it's not false humility.

It seems to me that parenting is a very private matter at the moment. Men talk about it much less than women on the whole, and to the extent that people do talk about it, they do so in a jokey way. They are reluctant to discuss their fears: are they too hard, too soft, too inconsistent?

It's noteworthy that while the papers are awash with advice about sexual relations, there's virtually nothing in them about people's parental relations, which is very odd considering that on the whole one leads to the other.

I am not trying to set up some system of adjudication of parenting but to create a more open environment in which people feel able to discuss what works and what doesn't. Not only do parents of teenage kids have lots of anxieties which they find difficult to discuss, but my guess is that everybody who has younger children has at some stage been shocked by the violence within themselves, when the kid is not sleeping or something. There is loads of advice about

182

how you deal with a baby up to about a year, and then it just tails away.

But I'm always aware of the dangers of moralising or criticising people's private lives, which I think is absolutely fatal for politicians, as witness the "Back to Basics" stuff.

You talk a lot about responsibilities, yet almost 50 per cent of eighteen- to thirty-four-year-olds say they would not be willing to sacrifice individual freedom in the public interest.

My guess is that the percentage has always been quite high, but it's probably got higher as a result of the experiences of the last sixteen years of a very acquisitive society, which has also discarded a lot of people. People think they've got to look after themselves.

We've got to get across to people that their own lives will be enriched if they feel they have a sense of obligation to other people. We're talking about enlightened self-interest, essentially. Societies can't function if people see rights simply as consumer possessions which have no downside to them. If people live in a functioning society, then apart from anything else they will enjoy more material benefits. They won't have to spend so much money on insurance, on dealing with the consequences of crime. Their children will have much more freedom; they'll be able to do what I could do when I was a kid and play for hours in a forest without coming to any harm. And since they're going to go through bad times as well as good, they will find that it's better to have a community around you that can support you, which is, after all, part of the purpose of the Health Service.

I can see that you can say to poor people, "There's something in it for you." But how are you going to persuade the rich and powerful, who see the poor as a threat, that by fulfilling their obligations they are going to benefit themselves?

In the same way the Victorian middle classes were sold public health in the last century: "Cholera has no boundaries." I think that's the best way to do it.

Are you optimistic that we are at a turning point?

Yes, I think we are. I think historians will say that a change was certainly necessary from the corporatist, collectivist ethos which had informed the country from 1940 through to the late Seventies, and it was desired by the British population. The mantle for that happened to fall on Mrs Thatcher. But that has now run its course. She shook things up, for sure, and not all that was done was bad, not by a long way; but we are now at an important moment of change.

I think that if we win the election, as I think we shall, the greatest burden on Tony Blair and the rest of us will not be delivering on the economy so much as the huge expectation that we will somehow be the agents of a different ethical order. That's going to be very difficult to handle, and the temptation to do it the old way will be very strong, but it is crucial that we resist this option.

Biography

Jack Straw was born in Essex in 1946 and educated at Brentwood School, Essex, and the University of Leeds, from which he graduated in 1967. He was president of Leeds University Union 1967–8 and president of the National Union of Students 1969–71.

He went to the Inns of Court School of Law, taking his Bar finals in 1972, and was called to the Bar in July of that year.

He practised as a barrister from 1972 to 1974. From 1971 to 1978 he was a member of Islington Borough Council. From 1971 to 1977 he was also a member of the Inner London Education Authority and from 1973 to 1974 was deputy leader of the ILEA.

He was special adviser to the Rt Hon. Barbara Castle, the Secretary of State for Social Services, from 1976 to 1977. From 1977 to 1979 he was on the staff of Granada Television's *World in Action*.

Since 1979 he has been the Member of Parliament for Blackburn.

He has served as the Opposition Treasury spokesperson and Opposition local government spokesperson. In 1987 he was elected to the shadow Cabinet, where he was first shadow Secretary of State for Education and then shadow Secretary of State for the Environment. He is currently shadow Home Secretary.

He is a regular contributor to *The Times*, the *Guardian*, the *Independent* and *Tribune* and has several publications to his name, including *Putting Blackburn to Work* (1993) and *Policy and Ideology* (1993).

Two interviews were conducted with Jack Straw on 23 January 1995 and 10 October 1995.